THE
MUSIC

THE PENGUIN
MUSIC
MAGAZINE

Edited by

RALPH HILL

I

PENGUIN
BOOKS
1946

PENGUIN BOOKS LIMITED
Harmondsworth, Middlesex, England

PENGUIN BOOKS INC.
245 Fifth Avenue, New York, U.S.A.

PUBLISHED DECEMBER 1946

MADE AND PRINTED IN GREAT BRITAIN
by Hazell, Watson & Viney Ltd.,
London and Aylesbury

CONTENTS

THROUGH THE LOOKING-GLASS: *Ralph Hill*   p. 7

THE FUTURE OF OPERA IN ENGLAND:
                                        Edward J. Dent   13

MUSIC INSPIRED BY PAINTING: *Michael Ayrton*   23

ANGLO-FRENCH RELATIONS: *Edward Lockspeiser*   29

SOVIET MUSIC IN WAR-TIME: *Alan Bush*   35

NEW-COMER TO MUSIC: *Cecil Elliott*   41

THE ORCHESTRA LOOKS AT THE AUDIENCE:
                                        Frederick Thurston   47

STANDARDS OF PERFORMANCE: *Geoffrey Sharp*   53

TO START AN ARGUMENT. I: WHAT IS THE
    PURPOSE OF MUSIC? *Scott Goddard and*
                                        C. B. Rees   60

PERSONALITY CORNER: *C. B. Rees*   69

BRAINS TRUST: *Julian Herbage*   75

NEW BOOKS: *Stanley Bayliss*   80

NEW MUSIC: *Robin Hull*   85

THE RECORD COLLECTOR: *Alec Robertson*   90

MUSIC ON THE AIR: *Richard Gorer*   95

OPERA IN LONDON: *Stephen Williams*   101

BALLET IN LONDON: *Arnold Haskell*   106

CONCERTS IN LONDON: *George Dannatt*   110

NORTHERN DIARY—
    Music in Scotland: *Stewart Deas*   116
    Music in Liverpool: *A. K. Holland*   119
    Music in Manchester: *J. H. Elliott*   121
    Music in Birmingham: *John Waterhouse*   124

Acknowledgment is made to the following
sources for the photographs used in the photo-
gravure plates : *Angus McBean*, pages 1, 2 and 3 ;
Baron Photo Centre Ltd., pages 6, 7 and 8 (bottom);
Richardby Photo Centre Ltd., page 8 (top);
Edward Mandinian, pages 9, 10 and 11 ; *Pictorial
Press*, page 12 ; *E.M.I.*, page 13 ; *London Phil-
harmonic Orchestra*, page 14 ; *Decca Record Co.,
Ltd.*, page 15 ; *B.B.C. London*, page 16.

THROUGH THE LOOKING-GLASS

Ralph Hill

FOREWORD

IT is customary for an author who has written a book on a popular subject to apologise to his readers for having brought into the world yet another book on the subject. However, I don't think there is any need for us to apologise for having produced a musical commentary, despite the fact that there are at least nine journals on this subject already safely established. Most of these are either specialised in their appeal or written primarily for professional musicians; while the *Penguin Music Magazine* is primarily written for amateurs. Once upon a time the word "amateur" referred specifically to a person who sang or played an instrument as a recreation and not as a means of livelihood. Such amateurs happily continue to exist to-day in fair numbers, but the executive ability of the vast majority of modern amateurs does not extend further than playing a gramophone. It is to this large and varied public, which neither descends to the "pin-up" appeal of comedian conductors nor yet ascends to the intellectual attractions of musicology, that we address ourselves.

The need for information and criticism of the right kind is obvious to all who have had experience of the gramophone societies and music clubs which flourish all over the country, and whose members represent the more alive and intelligent section of the amateur musical public at large. Writing in the *Sunday Times*, Gerald Abraham said that one obvious method of presenting such information and criticism is through musical journals and books "written not by professionals for professionals or by office-boys for the Tchaikovsky-sodden, but by professionals for the people who have just discovered Beethoven and

7

Brahms (*and* for the Tchaikovsky-sodden), by intelligent musicians who can write simply and interestingly and can show the new-comers the way about music without condescension or pedantry or vulgarity."

That, I think, sums up the aims of the *Penguin Music Magazine*. Thus we shall from time to time not only reflect and evaluate what has taken place in our world of music, but we shall discuss the problems confronting the new-comer to music. The two articles in this number "To Start an Argument" and "Brains Trust" are especially designed for the latter purpose. Readers are invited to send in suggestions for discussion.

A few words concerning some of the articles in the present issue. Since going to press Michael Ayrton has made some fresh researches into music inspired by painting, and we propose to publish, probably in the third issue, a continuation of Mr. Ayrton's article together with a supplement of reproductions of some of the pictures mentioned. C. Elliott, "New-comer to Music," and Frederick Thurston, "The Orchestra Looks at the Audience," break new ground. Mr. Elliott's work is far removed from the world of music, and he therefore speaks with a keenness and freshness of outlook that are salutary. Mr. Thurston, who was principal clarinet of the B.B.C. Symphony Orchestra from its inception, and is now devoting himself to solo work and chamber music, brings a new angle to the communal spirit of the public concerts. We all know what our reactions are to the orchestra, but this is probably the first time that we have ever heard what the orchestra's reactions are to us. J. H. Elliott, who gives us a picture of music in Manchester, records with pleasure that the Hallé Orchestra has returned to the air. Unfortunately the good news was short-lived. Some weeks later the B.B.C. refused to give the fee that the Hallé Society reasonably demanded for regular broadcasts. This matter I shall discuss at length in the next issue.

NEW CONCERT-HALLS

The need for concert-halls in London and the provinces is almost as pressing as the need for houses to live in. London has lost Queen's Hall; Manchester the Free Trade Hall; and Bristol Colston Hall. With the exception of a few places like Liverpool, Sheffield (where the acoustics of the City Hall are deplorable), and Wolverhampton, the existing halls—the Birmingham Town Hall is a good example—are inadequate in size and old-fashioned in equipment.

The lack of well-equipped civic halls throughout the country is a national disgrace. Before the war we flattered ourselves on our national commerce, but not on our national culture. Six years of war have made us begin to realise that to bring culture and healthy entertainment to the people, particularly young people, is as necessary as the provision of proper sanitation. The ill-nurtured mind can be potentially as dangerous as a stagnant sewer.

The civic hall should be the centre of culture and recreation in every city, town, and borough, a centre where both mental and physical culture are organised under the best conditions. And it can be done on a sure financial basis. Wolverhampton has proved that. The Wolverhampton Civic Hall is one of the two or three finest in the country, perhaps surpassed in internal architectural features only by the Liverpool Philharmonic Hall. In *Music in our Town: the Story of a Civic Hall*, which is a book that ought to be read by everyone interested in the possibilities of the civic hall, the authors, L. B. Duckworth and M. Bartlett-Hewitt, tell us that the project of building a hall in Wolverhampton had been talked about for thirty years and then considered for eight.

Nearly ten years later the project was put into effect, and finally the hall was completed in 1938. The opposition maintained that it would be a "white elephant" and "a further burden on the ratepayers." It is now an established and flourishing centre of music, drama, opera, and public dancing. The first year cost the rates £10,000, which spread over a population of some

113,000 worked out to less than two shillings per head. Five years later (1943-4) the cost had been reduced to £6,301.

The internal planning is excellent. The large hall, with its perfect acoustics, seats 1,780 and has platform accommodation for an orchestra of 80, a choir of 200, and a Compton four-manual organ. The small hall has a stage and seats 700. The two halls are linked by a refreshment-room that can accommodate 130 at tables. The Wolverhampton Civic Hall is a model for all future halls.

It is incredible that before the war London was served by only two concert-halls specifically designed for orchestral performances: the Queen's Hall, which was acoustically perfect but could seat only 2,500; and the Royal Albert Hall, which is full of acoustical distortion, but can accommodate 10,000 (the available accommodation is now, I believe, considerably smaller).

I maintain that London, with its enormous population and its prospects of becoming the cultural and political centre of Europe, makes a modern hall to seat 4-5,000 a vital necessity. In fact, London could easily do with three new halls—the Henry Wood Memorial Hall, a new Queen's Hall, and a really magnificent Civic Hall.

REVIVAL OF THE MUSIC FESTIVAL

Since the early eighteenth century the music festival has been one of the most important and sustaining influences in English music-making. The two outstanding characteristics of the English music festival are, first, that it does not exist for commercial ends, but merely to raise money for local charitable institutions; second, that its chief artistic purpose is to exploit the choral resources of the city and its surrounding districts.

English music has been rightly encouraged at English festivals, and many fine works that are now firmly established in the choral and orchestral repertoires were originally commissioned for a festival performance. But new works by distinguished foreign composers have also been given an important place in festival programmes.

Festivals have flourished (alas, some no longer exist), usually triennially, in Birmingham, Norwich, Leeds, and at the Crystal Palace, where gargantuan performances of Handel's oratorios used to be given. The oldest and most famous secular festival is that of the Three Choirs, which is held annually in turn at the three cathedral cities of Gloucester, Worcester, and Hereford. After a break of six years the Three Choirs Festival was revived at Hereford last month. We hope to publish a report of it in the future.

Two other festivals have taken place in England during the summer with great success—the Cheltenham Music Festival and the twentieth Festival of the International Society of Contemporary Music. The Cheltenham Festival is a new project, which deserves every support. The first, which consisted of three orchestral concerts by the London Philharmonic Orchestra under Dr. Malcolm Sargent, was given in 1945. These concerts were so successful that the Cheltenham Corporation was encouraged to extend the number of concerts to five (four orchestral concerts and one chamber-music concert) this year. The artistic policy is a progressive one, for the greater part of the programmes is devoted to works by British composers. A special attraction is the appearance in person of various composers as conductors of their own compositions. This year Bliss, Britten, Rubbra, Tippett, and Moeran were seen on the rostrum.

Of course, there has been the usual criticism of the die-hards, who know only what they like and like only what they know. They neither know nor like British music, or, in fact, any music that is not German in style or origin and of a vintage not fewer than fifty years old. Naturally, they want to see the programmes of the Cheltenham Festival devoted to the popular classics. The so-called festival designed on these lines may please the die-hards and may also fill the pockets of the get-rich-quick gentlemen who exploit the art of music for purely commercial ends, but it has no foundation in the true tradition of the English festival, which has both artistic and non-commercial aims.

I hope, therefore, the Cheltenham Corporation will treat these dissenters with the courteous contempt they deserve. If the Corporation will continue firmly with its present progressive policy, there is no reason why Cheltenham should not become an English Salzburg, which would bring international prestige to Cheltenham and to England as well.

Publisher's Note

One of the rarer definitions of the word Magazine is " a portable receptacle for articles of value," and we have taken the title Music Magazine for this publication in the hope that it will live up to this definition.   It is not a book, for its contents are more immediate than those of most books on music.   It is not a periodical, although we hope we may be able to refill the receptacle at some later date.

THE FUTURE OF OPERA IN ENGLAND

Edward J. Dent

*

ALL English musicians and music-lovers suffer more or less from an "inferiority complex" of long standing; a psycho-analyst could give it all sorts of new scientific names, and perhaps classify it under different types, according to the kind of music in which the patient was most interested. We like to think (as we did in 1880, and perhaps long before that) that we are now at last shaking it off, that our native composers are the equals, if not even the superiors, of any sort of foreigners, with orchestras and conductors to match, and choruses beyond all comparison. But these things are not the whole of the art and culture of music; if we are to form a correct general assessment, we must consider all forms of musical organisation, education, publishing, distribution of musical resources throughout the country, and many other aspects of musical activity.

One of the most important of these is opera; and on that subject the psycho-analyst might discover not merely a sense of inferiority but a sense of guilt and shame as well. "I will admit," says the imaginary intelligent foreigner, "that your country is not quite so utterly unmusical as I had been led to believe; but how is it that London, the wealthiest capital in Europe, does not possess and maintain an Opera on the scale and artistic level of Paris, Berlin, Vienna, or even Brussels, Copenhagen, and Stockholm?" We have a number of stock excuses ready, none of which is really valid, and we hope our foreign friend will accept them as a tolerant schoolmaster accepts the conventional excuses of his boys. But there is one stock answer to be heard now and then, and it is indeed a shameful one, all the more

13

shameful because it is generally given with an air of self-conscious virtue: "We are not an operatic nation; our people do not care for opera, they like serious music." The foreigner replies with grim politeness, "Ah, yes—the oratorios of Handel and Mendelssohn." In this connection I recall an observation made recently by one of our younger critics, that our vaunted choral singing is really the proof of our fundamental unmusicality, because any amateur can sing in a chorus, without ever taking the trouble to learn to sing at sight or to train his voice; the chorus is the refuge of the man who is too lazy to learn an instrument.

Opera, being a combination of several arts, is the most complex of all musical activities, so that in considering operatic history we must never lose sight of its history as an organisation, quite apart from its purely musical development as we may read it in the general histories of music. In Italy the history of opera is one continuous line from 1597 to the present day; in France the line is unbroken from 1672. But in Germany (including Austria) the line is for a very long time as erratic as it is in England; and we may take some encouragement from the thought that in the days of Weber (d. 1826) operatic conditions were not very different from what they were in England a hundred years later. The vast organisation of opera in Germany is just as much a product of the nineteenth century as the German railway system, and the railway system no doubt contributed to the operatic development.

In 1600 English intellectuals were probably a good deal more keenly interested in Italy than they are now, although travel to Italy was much more difficult. Inigo Jones could go to Italy and bring back drawings of scenery; a musician or two would bring back a parcel of Italian music. But designs for scenery and musical scores do not make an opera; an opera does not exist until we see it in action on the stage, and all through the seventeenth century there were not enough English travellers to Italy to bring back a really complete knowledge and understanding of what an opera was and how it was organised. It is notorious that in all artistic movements the English, living on a remote island, have been some fifty years or more behind the times. We made our first experiment in opera in 1656; but if any Italian saw *The Siege of Rhodes*, he must have thought it extremely out of date. After the Restoration it was comparatively easy to go to Paris, with the result that Restoration opera was organised mainly on French lines, although Purcell was very well read in Italian music. But Purcell never saw an Italian opera performed in Italy; at the most he may just possibly have read a full score— we know that Pepys possessed one, for it is in his library at Cambridge.

Apart from *Dido and Aeneas*, an experiment on a minute scale tried out in a girls' school and then discarded altogether, Purcell's "operas" are not operas at all in the accepted sense. In the reign of Queen Anne the practice of importing complete Italian opera began, and it remained the fashionable entertainment of the aristocracy for two hundred years. During those two centuries, whatever artistic heights it may occasionally have achieved in execution, it was essentially an assertion of wealth and social exclusiveness, and the same applies to the Italian opera which flourished in Paris, alongside of the national French opera, from about 1840 to 1870.

In the German countries the state of affairs was much the same throughout the eighteenth century; the only difference was that whereas in England the Italian opera was financed by the nobility and gentry with practically no subsidy from the Crown at all, in Germany it was mostly the private entertainment of the ruling princes. Native German opera, like native English opera, was popular but on the humblest level, and except in Italy, comic opera for the people, whether French, German, or English, really amounted to very little more than plays with songs. *The Beggar's Opera*, to name a familiar example, is typical, in that it is fundamentally a spoken play that would be quite a good play even if every note of music were cut out of it. German opera, as a national organisation, is a product of the German romantic movement which in every aspect of German life stressed the duty of being German to the core and abandoning all things foreign. The Italian opera survived longest in Vienna, always the most reactionary court of Europe.

The history of the spoken theatre in England during the nineteenth century is a chapter which none of us can read with any great sense of pride. A French critic, Augustin Filon, writing in 1896, said that the degradation of the English theatre was due largely to the English passion for music. The theatre simply reflected the general standards of education at the time; musical people may at least comfort their souls with the fact that just when the spoken theatre was at its lowest real English opera by native composers made an energetic start and developed into a school with a style of its own. *The Bohemian Girl* and *Maritana* may look rather faded to-day by the side of their contemporaries such as *Don Pasquale*, *Ernani*, *Rienzi*, and *Tannhäuser*, but the immense success of Balfe abroad shows that the general standard of operatic production was none too high anywhere in the 1840's. What is important in these Victorian days is not so much the production of native operas as the systematic performance of a general repertory in our own language instead of in Italian, and the establishment of a general understanding that foreign operas should be given in English more or less complete and unmutilated, instead of being "adapted" and ruthlessly rearranged as they were before about 1830. Throughout Queen Victoria's reign the demand for real opera in English steadily increased, and the foundation of the Carl Rosa company in 1875 is a significant landmark.

Opera reflected not merely the standard of education but also the social class-distinctions. We are only just now beginning to escape from the notion that no gentleman can possibly listen to opera in English.

At this moment we seem to be faced with the problem of building up opera again from the very foundations. It is a great piece of good fortune that Covent Garden escaped the war without damage. The house is there; what are we going to do with it? Starting to reconstruct our musical lives after six years of war, we inevitably look back to what happened after the previous war. The war of 1914 naturally put an end to the glories of old Covent Garden, the Covent Garden of the De Reszkes, of Melba and Caruso, with boxes all round the pit and grand tiers, and diamond tiaras in every one of them. Covent Garden became a furniture store; but Sir Thomas Beecham still carried on opera in English at the Shaftesbury and the Aldwych Theatres and after the war was over he established the British National Opera Company at Drury Lane. Its success was short-lived. Many of us hoped then that the British National Opera Company would develop into a permanent National Opera in English comparable to Paris and Berlin, but Covent Garden reopened, and from 1919 to 1939 it was again the home of international opera in foreign languages. But something else had happened, the historic importance of which few people can have grasped at that moment. It did not really matter very much if the Covent Garden performances were not quite so good as they were in King Edward's days; of course the elderly connoisseurs talked sadly of the Edwardian stars, just as the Edwardian connoisseurs talked about Grisi and Mario. The orchestra and the standard of performance as a whole were certainly on a far higher standard under Beecham. But the boxes were taken away, and the audience was different. The historic event, however, was at quite another theatre; it was the visit of the Russian Ballet under Diaghilev. The ballet, which in Victorian days had been considered something rather naughty, became a new religion, which affected all kinds of entertainment and indeed all kinds of social life. That it should attract smart society was only natural, but it became still more the artistic religion of the intellectuals; and it was indeed a religion, for within the ballet itself—not merely the Diaghilev ballet but all sorts of ballets, and especially in the Ballets Jooss and the Sadler's Wells ballet—there grew up insensibly what one can only call a religious devotion to the whole art of ballet. It is not just that any suggestion of "naughtiness" about ballet is now simply unthinkable; it is that ballet dancers, as far as one can judge, seem to take their art far more seriously than opera-singers do, and even far more seriously than most actors.

That is the real reason why ballet is now a far more popular entertainment than opera. Ballet has not been content with a lazy routine of worn-out conventions; it is continually advancing in technique and inventing new conceptions of choreography. And the Sadler's Wells ballet, while firmly rooted in the classics, has already evolved a definite English style. Its leaders are not content with the standards of the Continent; they have imagination enough to conceive of standards which nobody has ever seen realised anywhere.

What are we doing in opera? The most obvious sign of encouragement is *Peter Grimes*, a work of outstanding originality, quite unlike any other modern opera, and an opera which has confronted its producers and performers—and its audiences too —with new problems, new standards, and a new outlook altogether. Up till now we have never had any really high standard of English operatic performance, despite one or two exceptional productions at rare intervals. No one, not even the experts, has ever seen a performance of opera in English, let alone of a native opera, up to the normal standards of Paris, Berlin, and Dresden. This is not a matter of individual voices but of opera as a whole, taking every detail into consideration, including all those minute yet indispensable details which the average operagoer hardly notices. The achievement of such a standard depends of course largely on finance, and also on voices, but what is most important of all is the combination of brains, imagination, and endless capacity for taking trouble.

The gist of all Bernard Shaw's criticisms on the music of London fifty years ago was that we never took music seriously enough. If we are to achieve a National Opera on the highest level, we must take a great deal more trouble over every detail than we have ever taken before. The result of our having no really English standards is that most people, opera-managers, singers, conductors, critics, and audiences, inevitably form their judgments by foreign standards. France, Germany, and Italy have each a huge repertory of native standard operas as a foundation of their style, although all these countries perform foreign operas in translations. Here we have practically no native repertory. *The Bohemian Girl* and *Maritana* have by now dropped out almost entirely; the operas of Stanford, Gatty, Vaughan Williams, and Boughton, despite their indisputable distinction, have never become regular repertory operas, familiar to the public at large. A French, German, or Italian theatre could if necessary carry on perfectly well with native operas alone; any English company is forced to depend on foreign works. That was exactly the German situation in the days of Mozart, Beethoven, and Weber; Weber as a conductor had just as much difficulty in getting his German audiences to swallow Mozart and Beethoven as any English manager has now in popularising Stanford and Vaughan Williams.

Our stock repertory, like Weber's, is mainly Italian and French, and in addition to that we are still haunted by the Italian tradition of Victorian days when all operas, including French and German, were habitually sung in Italian. Everybody calls the operas by their foreign names, even when these are not names of characters —*Trovatore, Tabarro, Meistersinger, Rosenkavalier*—instead of translating them as the French do. Singers learn favourite songs in Italian to sing at concerts, and generally prefer to have them recorded in Italian. If they have to sing the opera on the stage in English, they try to make it sound as much like Italian as possible. The modern public becomes acquainted with opera largely through gramophone records and hence forms an entirely false idea of it. A singer who makes a record naturally wants to assert her own voice and personality, to be recognised as Miss X, not to create the illusion that the listener is looking at Butterfly or Mimi on the stage. I can understand the point of view of the connoisseurs who want to hear all operas in their original languages, though I find that many of them seem quite indifferent as to how those languages may be pronounced, and I am myself wholeheartedly on the side of those who want all operas in their own language; but I cannot understand those who seem to prefer English to be made to sound as much like Italian as possible. If we are to have Italian, let it be real Italian, not German-Italian, Czech-Italian, or English-Italian; if English, let it sound like the King's English as we expect to hear it in Shakespeare. The stock argument against English is that all translations are ludicrously bad. Very well then, let us set to work to improve them. The English translations current are no worse than the current French, German, and Italian translations of foreign operas. It is true that many original librettos are bad; but not so many as people who have never studied them imagine, and a bad libretto can often be a good deal improved by free translation. It is absurd to say that English is of itself a bad language for opera; people say that because they judge it by translated operas. Set the foreign operas aside for a moment and ask yourself if you would prefer to hear *Peter Grimes* sung in Italian.

The present management of Covent Garden has firmly made up its mind to create a national English opera company singing all operas in English. It will cordially welcome occasional visits from complete foreign ensembles, but it will have nothing more to do with the old system of what has been called "a pedigree herd" of foreign stars from various countries with any hotch-potch scenery that can be put up out of stock, and with leading British singers in minor parts in any language as long as it is not English. The Editor of this magazine asks me to discuss " the vexed question of whether the German and Italian repertoire should or should not be sung in English." What about the French and Russian repertory? Is that not equally important? By all means let us invite a complete French or Russian company to London for a three or four weeks' visit; but who nowadays wants to hear *Eugene Onegin* in Italian, *Armide* in German, or

Tannhäuser in French, as I have myself heard them at Covent Garden in bygone years? Some audiences will even tolerate mixed languages; but I remember with delight a performance of *Lohengrin* at Brussels with a German Lohengrin (an excellent singer) who on his first entrance addressed the King in German, to which the King, following the accepted French version, replied "Merci, j'ai bien compris." The whole house roared with laughter.

I cannot think that there is more than a handful of people who would like to see opera for the rich at Covent Garden in foreign languages and opera for the poor in English at Sadler's Wells. What I should like to see is two really national opera houses as in Paris, both singing in our own language, both on the highest artistic level, and dividing the operatic repertory according to size, large and spectacular operas such as *Aida, Meistersinger,* and *Rosenkavalier* at Covent Garden, smaller and more intimate operas such as *Marriage of Figaro, Barber of Seville,* and *Bartered Bride* at Sadler's Wells. The two repertories would correspond to those of the Paris Opéra and Opéra-Comique, except that there would probably be more overlapping. What the future may bring will depend on the general economic and social conditions of England. The faded Victorian glamour of Covent Garden Theatre must not tempt us to imagine that we can ever recover the legendary glories of the age of Grisi and Mario; Queen Victoria is no less dead than Queen Anne. We must make a fresh start with altogether new ideals, and we must train up our younger generation—composers, singers, conductors, producers, designers, and audiences too—systematically towards these ideals. We cannot train these young people unless we can make opera a real and honourable career, and that involves establishing national opera not only in London, but in Manchester, Glasgow, Leeds, Birmingham, and as many more separate centres as we can achieve. Only then will it be possible for singers to concentrate entirely upon opera, not regarding it as they mostly do now, as a side issue, and making their living mainly out of oratorio and broadcasting. As long as they do that, they are constantly wanting to be away from the theatre and missing rehearsals, which means that it is impossible to raise the general standard of operatic performance. There has been much talk of establishing a new national school for operatic training, but I am sceptical as to its value under present conditions. The trouble with the existing schools of music is not that their teaching is inadequate, but that they cannot in common humanity advise students to concentrate exclusively on a type of work which is economically precarious. The general public attaches an exaggerated importance to large and powerful voices. What most of our singers need is more cultivation of general intelligence, more musicianship, better pronunciation of their own language, more literary understanding, and, generally speaking, more ability to apply their brains to the solution of any problem, vocal, literary, dramatic, or musical, that they may have to encounter. Nor must we forget the urgent necessity for training character, which includes the sense of artistic integrity, loyalty to the theatre and towards colleagues, as well as the psychological insight required for the presentation of many different personalities in musical drama.

Hubert Parry once wrote that "opera is the shallowest fraud man ever achieved in the name of art." Parry, born in 1848, was brought up in that Victorian upper class which delighted in Donizetti at Her Majesty's; we cannot be surprised at this judgment from a man of his moral and artistic ideals. I, as one of those who entered musical life on the crest of the great Wagnerian wave of the 1890's, would maintain that opera is, or ought to be, the highest possible manifestation of music and the sister arts. The younger generation of to-day, being as much obsessed with Puccini as the generation of 1846 was with Donizetti, seems to be quite unaware of opera as a profound spiritual experience. To that experience our young composers must lead us back, and it is they who must inspire our singers, as Wagner did his, and all who work in the theatre, with a sense of self-dedication to the service of the community.

MUSIC INSPIRED BY PAINTING

Michael Ayrton

*

THE non-musical aspect of the composer's inspiration apparent
in programme music, composed on specific subjects, has led
many composers to pay passing tribute to the other arts. Quite
apart from opera, which is not within the scope of this article
and where the link is more obviously definable, the romantic
trend towards programme music in the early nineteenth
century provoked a spate of orchestral music directly resulting
from emotions derived both from painting and literature.
Literature naturally played the largest part. The works of
Shakespeare and Byron were indirectly responsible for numerous
overtures and symphonic poems, whilst the figure of Faust
seems to have been musically almost inescapable during the
first half of the nineteenth century. In a lesser degree painting
played its part in the creation of the romantic movement, though
this particular aspect seems to have been of more interest to
Liszt than to Berlioz, Weber, and the other major figures of
the time. There is indeed a considerable quantity of Liszt's work
directly derived from the visual arts.

During his stay in Rome in 1838–39, and influenced by his
friendship with the painter Ingres, Liszt turned to painting as
a source of inspiration. He was so deeply moved by the sculpture
and painting of the great Renaissance artists that he even drew
unlikely parallels between their work and the products of his
own art, going so far indeed as to compare Rossini with Titian.
Inspired by Michelangelo, Liszt composed *Il Penseroso* and, after
seeing a Raphael at Milan, he wrote his equally celebrated
Sposalizio. Both these latter were fantasias comprising part of

the extensive collection of picturesque piano pieces, which he called "Les Années de Pelerinage" (The Years of Pilgrimage). These are both relatively gentle works, but the best of Liszt's pictorially inspired compositions seem to motivate from the more gloomy and savage examples of the visual arts.

In the Campo Santo at Pisa, unless it is now destroyed by the bomb-induced fires of the Italian campaign, is the fresco by Andrea Orcagna called the "Triumph of Death." This mighty picture shows Death, in the figure of a woman flying, on bat's wings, through a great landscape. She reaps the corpses of kings and nobles, of beggars and cripples, of old and young, with a scythe held in her taloned figures. Her hair streams in the wind and her clothes are crusted with filth. The souls of the slain are received from these new-mown cadavers either by radiant angels or by the devil-tended fires. This picture inspired Liszt to write that superb and curiously neglected fantasia for piano and orchestra, the *Todtentanz*. His musical treatment of this terrible subject takes the form of a set of variations on the central theme of a majestic "Dies Irae," which is introduced at the outset by the orchestra. The theme is restated on the piano so that it becomes, with its diabolic *glissandi*, a sickeningly rapid death march, merciless and inescapable, the whole containing the very essence of mortality. There is one tranquil passage charged with hope, and then the fiends of hell take over. It is of particular interest, for it is one of the rare examples of a great picture producing its counterpart in great music.

Undoubtedly the visual arts served Liszt as emotional material to a far greater extent than any other great composer. At least two of his major orchestral works derive directly from pictorial sources, and the piano piece *Il Penseroso* was later arranged for orchestra as *La Notte*, one of the three *Odes Funèbres*. *Orpheus*, a symphonic poem still in the general repertoire, was partly inspired by an Etruscan vase painting, and among Liszt's works less frequently performed, *St. Francis of Paolo* was suggested by a drawing by E. J. von Steinle, and *Von der Wiege bis zum Grabe* resulted from Liszt's admiration for a deplorable sketch by Count Michael Zichy.

It is perhaps odd that a composer as sensitive as Liszt should have been so indiscriminate in his pictorial tastes. No one would dream of disputing Michelangelo, Raphael, and Orcagna as worthy of musical homage, but Liszt seems to have waxed equally enthusiastic about the third-rate von Steinle and the vague amateurism of Count Michael Zichy. The explanation must be that either Liszt's taste was ludicrously uneven or, a more hopeful and likely alternative, the very weakness of bad pictures gives greater scope for musical interpretation and expansion than the pictorial masterpiece.

Certainly of the body of music inspired by pictures, the outstanding musical achievement has, in two major instances, been inspired by the most prosaic painting. *Die Hunnenschlacht*, one of Liszt's most striking and all too rarely performed symphonic poems, derived from a monumentally large and dull battle-piece by the fervid German academic, Ernst von Kaulbach. Indeed, so moved was Liszt by the grandiose epic of this academic bore, that he proposed a whole cycle of symphonic poems based on Kaulbach's vast and solemn daubs, to be entitled "The History of the World in Sound and Picture." The fact that Liszt was moved to compose as much by seeing the work of Kaulbach and Zichy as by that of Michelangelo and Orcagna also leads one to suppose that subject, rather than treatment, came first in his interest.

It is also to be presumed that it was subject rather than pictorial excellence which encouraged Mussorgsky to take what must have been a depressing promenade through Hartmann's exhibition. The quality of those "Pictures in an Exhibition" which so moved Mussorgsky to such splendid music is of a very low order.

On the other hand, two second-rank works, the picture by the once famous Swiss artist Boecklin called the "Isle of the Dead," and the composition derived from it by Rachmaninov, set each other off very successfully, perhaps because the prime ingredient of both the painting and the music is melodrama. Rachmaninov's symphonic poem is an example of the preoccupation with morbid painting in which composers seem to indulge. The music in this case is almost exactly as good as the painting, which means that the latter is considerably better than current fashion esteems it. The picture itself is of a lonely Mediterranean island, rocky and overgrown with cypresses, to which a boat manned by shrouded figures is gliding over motionless water. The dramatic impact of the painting is considerable, for, with a masterly academic technique and a minimum of grisly props, the artist has conveyed a sense of utter lifelessness.

The gloomy, Swiss, near-surrealism of Boecklin also provided Max Reger with musical subject-matter. Reger was responsible for no fewer than four dreary tone poems named after equally depressing pictures by Boecklin, one of which is another version of "The Isle of the Dead," though to my mind none of them rank with Rachmaninov's achievement. I must, however, admit to having heard the Reger only once and then only in a piano version.

The dramatic, romantic, even necrophilist, element in painting seems to have proved peculiarly alluring to the musician, and one might have expected El Greco, Peter Breughel, Jerome Bosch, Urs Graf, Callot, or more the lurid elements of Signorelli to prove irresistible to the composer of a "Freischütz," a "Fantastic" Symphony or a "Wozzeck." In actual fact, one of the several piano pieces on paintings by that underrated Czech composer Zdenek Fibich, a highly effective work called *Carnaval and Lent* is the only musical reaction to Breughel's art of which I am aware. It is a savage and at the same time genial interpretation of one of the Flemish master's celebrated pictures.

Callot has received one tribute, that of William Walton's *Scapino* overture, which, though somewhat violent, is mainly in light sardonic vein, whilst Greco, Bosch, Graf, and Signorelli have not, so far as I know, found any musical interpretation as yet. It is interesting and perhaps surprising that Walton, both in *Scapino* and in the overture after a water-colour by Rowlandson, "Portsmouth Point," has chosen gay aspects of the work of these two frequently savage draughtsmen.

Mathias Grünewald, greatest and most terrible of all the Gothic mystic painters, has been paid musical tribute on the largest scale of all. Hindemith composed an entire opera—*Mathis der Mahler*—about him; and subsequently a symphony in three movements on Grünewald's *chef d'œuvre*, the Isenheim polyptych at Colmar. Each movement of the symphony bears the title of a part of the great altar-piece, which contains ten separate panels, combining to create as a whole one of the highest achievements in the whole art of painting. The first is concerned with the left-hand inner panel, a concert of angels, represented in strange spectromatic colours, playing on various stringed instruments to the Madonna and Child. The second movement describes the Entombment painted on the predella, whilst the third is a musical version of one of the outer wings, the "Temptation of St. Anthony," in which the poor old gentleman is beset by frightful demons and creatures half beast, half human, in a setting of desolate rocks and ruins. The music is in no sense a counterpart of the mighty creation of Grünewald—I doubt if anything by a lesser composer than Beethoven possibly could be—but it is, on a different scale, an interesting work, well scored and, perhaps because of the dramatic content of the subject, in the last movement particularly successful and exciting.

I am well aware that in this article I have been able to mention few examples of music of the very first rank, and perhaps it might be inferred that the effect of painting on music is not greatly to be admired. This may well be true, but equally I have cited many works well worth writing and hearing. For though there is no real link between the two arts, they together constitute a major part of man's immortality, and where they meet in tributes one to another they merit consideration.

In a further series of notes, which will appear in a subsequent issue, I will attempt to deal with those composers who were inspired by painting of a gentler kind, and also to remark on several more of Liszt's compositions which have recently come to my attention. These latter were inspired—if it is conceivable— by even worse pictures than some of those already mentioned in connection with Liszt. I therefore hope to augment the final instalment with a supplement of illustrations covering the range of both articles. This supplement will, if anyone can be induced to photograph them, contain some of the worst pictures ever reproduced.

ANGLO-FRENCH
RELATIONS

Edward Lockspeiser

*

I THINK it was Busoni who once shrewdly observed that in everyone's conception of the art of music there flowed the River Rhine. He meant to say that there was the Latin conception and the Teutonic conception, and that these represented two civilisations, sometimes opposed to each other, sometimes merged or intertwined, but always distinguishable, and, by the very nature of the conflict between them, always productive. Busoni's observation was of course an over-simplification of this geographical view of music which, in any case, was neither particularly new nor original. It is, however, a view that is about to present itself to us again in a new form and which no one who is interested in the progress of music can afford to ignore. I mean that as we emerge, now, from a long period of artistic isolation we need to be reminded that it is precisely by the action and influence of the music of one country upon that of another that progress is maintained. For whatever may be said for economic or political isolation, artistic isolation leads to parochialism and eventually to sterility. The curtain is about to go up on the new European scene; artistic intercourse is slowly being re-established between the nations. Musicians from many European countries have visited England, while numerous English musicians have travelled abroad. The machinery of the concert world has by no means returned to normal, and our knowledge of the trends and tendencies of the new composers abroad is still scanty. But the main point is that we are no longer barred and bolted against each other. We may open our minds, now, to a fresh and regenerating stimulus and in return hope to provide our own contribution to future developments in the post-war musical world.

We have already done so to some extent. One of the important things one notices in the French musical world to-day is the interest, quite genuine and not arising from any sort of national propaganda, in modern English music. This is a new manifestation, for, as everyone knows, the French were long inclined to sniff at our music (with the solitary exception of Purcell), to misspell the names of English composers, sometimes to the extent of parodying them, and generally to delight in an almost complete ignorance of what was going on across the Channel, as if all we had achieved amounted to some provincial or amateurish activity. The French, we said by way of self-defence, were much more insular than ourselves; and while, here, we continued to watch the French developments very closely—I am speaking of the 1920's and 30's—often giving a place in our programmes to works which were really quite unexportable, we came to accept the fact that between the two countries there was to be little or no musical interchange.

All this is now changed. And for some very obvious reasons. In the first place the French seem to have come to the end of what, as we see now, was a Golden Age in their music. It was perhaps only natural that at a time when not only the French school itself was extremely active, but when composers from Central Europe, Spain, Italy, and Russia all regarded Paris as a clearing-house for their works—it was only natural that the French critics caught up in this feverish activity should have had little time for the milder idealism of modern English music. If they did admire a contemporary English composer, it was generally because of his unEnglish qualities, e.g. Lord Berners or earlier Cyril Scott. The unmistakably English qualities of Elgar eluded them completely. As they listened to the Enigma Variations they thought only of the influences of César Franck or Tchaikovsky and were unable to imagine how such a work could represent the spirit of Victorian or Edwardian England.

Vaughan Williams similarly received no recognition in France. He represented to the French musician merely a belated expression of nationalism and belonged, in his view, to the category of composers including Dvořák and Grieg. The mysticism of Holst suggested Wagner, his exoticism the Russians. Delius was a misplaced Romantic. Here, then, as they looked at the picture of our music—if indeed they took the trouble to look at all—were a host of different tendencies which they were unable to correlate, and they made no further effort to define the character of our music as a whole, in its broad national aspects.

I think that enlightened French musicians, in the retrospective mood to which they seem to be given nowadays, are anxious to explore this by-passed territory of modern English music. It so happens that there are at least two composers who, temperamentally and artistically, appeal to them: I am referring to Walton and Britten, many of whose works have met with as great a success in France as in England. The same is true of several works of Rawsthorne and Tippett. Concerts of modern English music in France—unheard of before the war—are now listened to with curiosity, discernment, and appreciation. Nor is this newly awakened interest confined to the most recent developments. Across this bridge, so to speak, the more inquiring minds are anxious to investigate the hinterland of English music. Of course they are going to be extremely fastidious; and we may trust them to ferret out all sorts of "influences," more disturbing, perhaps, to the analytical French mind than to our own. But certain distinctive features are at last apparent to them, and I think there is a tendency to readjust their judgments.

Ever since the influence of Rossetti and the Pre-Raphaelites on Debussy—an influence that was by no means negligible in his formation—the French have expected to see some reflection of the main æsthetic trends of modern English literature in English music. Cultured French people have often a good knowledge of modern English literature and expect to see some family resemblance between the work of our writers and composers.

It is there, easily discernible. Whitman, Housman, the Sitwells, and Auden are among the poets who have each their musical counterparts, and it would be interesting for some student to attempt to define these literary influences: it would be a study attractive to ourselves as well as to the French, for whom music is an art much more closely associated with literature than in other countries. It is precisely here that a composer with such an alert literary sense as Britten makes his appeal. I am not suggesting that this is the only appeal of Britten, or that the purely musical merit of any composer foreigners choose to admire should not be sufficient in itself; I am merely referring to an aspect of English music that may lead to a closer understanding of our contribution.

Now for the other side of the picture. The cause of French music in England has long been won. There was a time, in fact, when it seemed that the individuality of English composers was likely to be distorted or submerged by their enthusiasm for the revelations of Debussy and Ravel, as earlier the threat had come from Wagner and the Russians and earlier still from Mendelssohn and Brahms. The progress of Walton from his early and somewhat Ravelian *Façade* to the Violin Concerto; a comparison of Vaughan Williams's *On Wenlock Edge*, written shortly after his return from France, with his later choral and instrumental works, or of Bliss's early *Rout* with his *Pastoral*—comparisons such as these show that the character of English music has been able to define itself and to absorb, rather than to be distorted by, foreign influences. There were, of course, many —Strauss and Debussy, Hindemith and Stravinsky, and more recently Sibelius, and still others from Central Europe and Russia, with the result that one aspect of modern English music was almost a battleground on which these contending personalities strove for supremacy. I think that the emergence from all these cosmopolitan trends of such a characteristically national figure as Vaughan Williams is as remarkable a phenomenon as the emergence in France, half a century ago, of Debussy. The national profile in the work of these composers is unmistakable. They are personalities who have not only become mature; they have become themselves.

It is a curious fact that to-day we have less knowledge of the most recent French composers than we had of corresponding figures a generation ago. The acquaintance of most people stops with the work of Poulenc and Sauguet. But what has been written in France during and since the war? One is struck by the fact that while the poems of Eluard and Aragon are widely discussed, while there is no dearth of articles explaining the "existentialism" of Jean-Paul Sartre, while the pictures of Matisse, Braque, and Rouault are exhibited at famous galleries, there has been little opportunity of hearing the most recent French music. Many French conductors have visited England since the war, but their programme has for the most part been strangely unadventurous. Until the I.S.C.M. Festival, Ibert and Messiaen were the only leading French composers introduced into their programme and neither of them by representative works.

Messiaen is the composer in France to-day who has provoked the most controversy—the French musical world would not be itself without a strong current of controversy—and a band of admirers believe in him as a *chef d'école*. He is an organist and a teacher of composition at the Paris Conservatoire. Nearly all his works are inspired by religious subjects, bearing such titles as *Visions de l'Amen, Vingt regards de l'Enfant Jésus, Trois Petites Liturgies*. Messiaen prefaces these works with long explanations of their religious message, often in rather questionable taste. His style is extremely decorative and improvisatory, but the under-lying sentiment would seem to be less an expression of religious mysticism than an echo, heavily disguised, of Massenet or Gounod. André Jolivet, belonging to the same generation, similarly cultivates a complex style, as in his *Five Ritual Dances*, but shows more affinity with Roussel and Stravinsky. Of an older generation Henry Barraud is much more discreet—to use a word beloved of French critics—and still believes in that highly prized concept across the Channel, "the economy of means." Roland-Manuel, in his Piano Concerto among other works, perpetuates the tradition of his master, Ravel. Pierre Capdevielle is something of a musical philosopher, while Daniel Lesur, on the other hand, harks back to Chabrier. There are two women composers, Elsa Barraine and Claude Arrieu, who seem to be something more than accomplished. There are the young experimentalists, Serge Nigg, André Casanova, and René Leibowitz. And the list may be extended to include several foreign composers for whom France is a spiritual home. We owe it to ourselves to be at least aware of the activities of these new French composers and to welcome the best of them to play their part in music's fructification.

SOVIET MUSIC IN WAR-TIME

Alan Bush

*

AT 4 a.m. on Sunday, June 22nd, 1941, Hitler's armies invaded the Soviet Union. The Red Army sprang to its defence. With equal promptitude the musicians started to organise themselves alongside the Red Army and their fellow-citizens of the Union. A conference of composers and writers was called in Moscow on the afternoon of that very first day of the war. Its agenda was to discuss how musicians could most effectively aid the war effort. Its immediate result was the production of more than one hundred topical songs, which were written, composed, published, and given the very widest publicity through the Press and the Radio within seven days. They were songs designed for singing by Red Army men, by concert-parties, professional and amateur, in fact by everybody for everybody, songs with serious, optimistic, realistic texts, musically straightforward in character, easy to learn and easy to understand by the widest public. From that beginning the energies of the Soviet musical world were increasingly directed to the task of fighting the invader. Compositions of all kinds, from those simple mass-songs to full-length cantatas, symphonies, and operas, have poured forth from the Soviet composers and have been given immediate and frequent performances. Directly or indirectly, these musical works have reflected the experiences of the people of the Soviet Union as they repelled the onslaughts of the Nazi military machine, whose guts they tore out, in the graphic words of Mr. Churchill.

How was this feat of organisation achieved? In the initial stages by the efforts of the musicians themselves, and especially by the composers and writers on music, organised in the Union of Soviet Composers.

This organisation, which dates from the year 1932, was designed to unite all composers and writers on music who were actively engaged in work which promoted the cultural progress of the people in general. At the same time it emphasised the freedom of stylistic tendencies, and proclaimed the principle of creative freedom for the artist, while at the same time preserving the right of all its members to criticise all artistic productions. The 300 applications for membership received at its inception were critically examined, and 150 finally accepted, as the remainder did not meet the requirements of genuine professionalism.

The main work of the Union has been to promote the composition of new works, and to publicise them in every possible way. Large funds were placed at the disposal of the Union, and they were expended in commissions to composers, to promoting concerts of Soviet music, to improving the living conditions of composers, encouraging their further education, and to providing a meeting-place where they could meet and discuss their problems, together with the musicologists and general musical public of the Soviet Union as a whole.

The Union of Soviet Composers, in association with the Council of People's Commissars (one of the main executive organs of the Government), worked out scales of fees for commissions to composers as follows: for opera, 10,000 to 12,000 rubles; symphony, 6,000 to 8,000 rubles; chamber works, 3,000 to 5,000 rubles, and so forth with differential payments depending upon the type of work. These amounts were paid to the composer in instalments during the time he was engaged upon actually composing the work. In this way new compositions could be embarked upon without the financial embarrassments which the necessities of living otherwise impose upon the composer. The amounts paid out in this way have increased from the first year of the existence of the Union of Soviet Composers until 1943 (the last datum which is available on the subject). In 1932, twelve composers received in all 15,000 rubles; in 1940, forty composers received 70,000 rubles, while in 1943 the number had risen to one hundred composers, who received 100,000 rubles. The membership of the Union has risen accordingly from its original beginnings with 150 members, to 450 in 1939, and over 800 to-day.

The problems with which the Union of Soviet Composers had to deal brought about by war-time conditions were many, from purely creative problems to those dealing with the organisation of air-raid defence and military training. The Præsidium of the Organisational Committee met daily at the beginning of the war for many months on end. Special funds were set up; firstly a fund of 750,000 rubles for forming concert-parties to be sent to the front-line units and mobilisation centres, and it was decided that each brigade of concert-parties should include a composer among its members; secondly, a fund of 750,000 rubles for commissioning the writing of music with special relevance to the war situation; thirdly, a fund of 200,000 rubles for aiding evacuated composers; fourthly, a fund of 300,000 rubles for aiding the families of composers who had enlisted in the Popular Guards; fifthly, a fund of 500,000 rubles for maintaining a Pioneer Camp for the children of evacuated composers.

During the first months of the war the majority of the Moscow and Leningrad composers remained in their homes and continued their work there. Some were called up into the army, others enlisted in the Popular Guards. Several met their death fighting at the front. The families of Moscow and Leningrad composers were evacuated to the Urals. By a decision of the Council of People's Commissars, the Organisational Committee of the Union of Soviet Composers was evacuated from Moscow in October 1941.

Very shortly after the outbreak of the war, the Soviet Government began to pay great attention to the needs of composers under war-time conditions. First, they made arrangements for the evacuation of composers far into the interior, where they could go on with their creative work in a relatively undisturbed atmosphere. Many, though not all, composers took advantage of this. Some preferred to remain in cities such as Moscow and Leningrad, where they were in the front line of defence. Composers were listed on a special military register and granted long-term exemption from mobilisation. A special order regulated rationing supplies for composers.

Many conferences have been held throughout the war, the first being in Moscow in April 1942, in which a review of the composers' work in the preceding ten months was surveyed. In a resolution adopted at this meeting it was agreed, among other things, that "The award in 1941 of Stalin Prizes to five composers —Alexandrov, Khrennikov, Mshvelidze, Shostakovich, and Zakharov—testifies to the fact that the Soviet people and the Soviet Government appreciate the contribution of Soviet composers to the common cause of fighting against Nazism, that Soviet composers, despite the difficulties of war-time, are bearing aloft the banner of Soviet art, as are all Soviet workers, and that they will win Soviet art new victories by creating works of national and world significance."

Shostakovich, who was awarded a Stalin Prize in 1941 for his Piano Quintet, was to receive a further award for his Seventh Symphony, the *Leningrad*. In this work, the first three movements of which were written in Leningrad itself during the severest autumn and winter months of the siege, the composer sought to express in symphonic form the experience of a happy and united people visited with the hideous calamity of the fascist invasion and fighting their way to triumph despite unimaginable sufferings. The people felt their immediate emotions and aspirations powerfully and intelligibly portrayed. They responded with an outburst of popular enthusiasm such as can rarely, if ever, have been accorded to the first performance of any symphonic orchestral work since the lifetime of Beethoven. Shostakovich indeed achieved much in developing the love and understanding of the Soviet people for their composers, and advanced their appreciation of the art of music in general by the creation of this remarkable composition, an aspect of his achievement which is not always appreciated elsewhere.

Energetic measures were taken in the rehabilitation of the musical life of the regions devastated by the invasion immediately the Nazis were driven out. Already ten Conservatoires of Music are functioning in the territories overrun by the Nazi armies, with a total of 1,700 students during the present academic year. The total number of students in music institutions of all types throughout the Union, including a large number in the autonomous Republics of Georgia, Armenia, Azerbaijan, Kazakhstan, and Uzbekistan, is 63,500. These range from the special Schools for Talented Children, through elementary and secondary music schools to the twenty conservatoires. Throughout the war musical education went on for people of all ages, professional and amateur. The opera-houses continued their work, though the main Moscow and Leningrad companies were evacuated to the interior.

Many new operas were composed and produced, among others the *War and Peace* of Prokofiev. Notable operatic productions from other countries included *Porgy and Bess*, by George Gershwin, which was very well received by the Moscow public. Many concerts of the music of the United Nations have been given. Concerts of British, American, Polish, Czech, and French music have been quite frequent. The general impression is one of immense activity organised with lavish financial support from the exchequer, and enjoying the enthusiastic backing of an enormous public.

The reconstruction and development of musical life has already started apace. Opera-houses and concert-halls are being rebuilt or built afresh in the devastated towns. Professional and amateur activity has already redoubled its vast war-time extent. Musical education, free except for a few of the highest institutes, where a very small percentage of the costs are met by fees from such students as can afford to pay, is reaching out to ever wider circles of the people. The manufacture of musical instruments has greatly increased, and within a short time the setback which the invasion inevitably caused in some aspects of musical life will have been overcome, and activity more widespread than ever before will enrich the lives of the people of the Soviet Union. No wonder that the Soviet Union is so jealous a guardian of the peace of the world, and so anxious that the forces of fascism be not permitted again to raise their heads in any corner of Europe or of the world, and thus endanger the peace, which has been bought by such heroism and sacrifice as the history of man does not equal in any past period.

NEW-COMER TO MUSIC

Cecil Elliott

*

MANY reasons have been given to account for the greatly increased interest in music during the last decade. The war, which
created a psychological reaction of one kind or another, is given
by some observers as a possible cause. It is not my purpose to
question this, but being a new-comer to more attentive listening
to serious music, both in the concert-hall and over the air, I feel
my growing interest was not the result of tiring war years, but
the necessity of a maturing mind, or the seriousness of fast-
approaching middle age—perhaps both.

I reflect now on the wasted years with a sense of disappointment.
Remembering the times I have listened with tolerance to so-called
light musical programmes, and the tenor-soprano act singing
musical comedy, I realise with some feeling of frustration how
much real musical pleasure I have missed. And how much I am
still losing, in certain respects, in my very disorganised chase
through a maze of beauty; missing, as it were, so much of this
elusive beauty in pursuit of wasted time. How many other people
are there in the same dilemma as myself? I would suggest the
vast majority of listeners and concert-goers. I am making this
assumption from the fact that concerts have better attendances
when works of a nature more easily understood are being performed. A concert that includes Tchaikovsky's Piano Concerto
in B flat minor attracts bigger audiences than would a concert in
which the concerto is in D minor and is by Brahms.

Why does the average concert-goer avoid unfamiliar paths and
keep to the well-worn track?

I suggest that the answer is that the majority of listeners cannot
afford to be explorers. Concert-going is an expensive entertainment compared with the cinema, consequently the average con-

cert-goer can only afford to hear what he can be sure of enjoying.
Thus he runs the risk, as I have done, of getting into a rut and
remaining content to listen only to the bigger and better-known
symphony orchestras playing only the well-known repertoire
conducted by some well-known conductor. This may be all very
well for the box-office, but it must end in musical stagnation.
It is not prejudice that arrests the wider appreciation of musical
art, but the pecuniary wherewithal to venture into the unknown.

Art for art's sake might be one of the answers to this question,
but even music-lovers are obliged to eat.

I admit that the B.B.C. brings every kind of music to our very
firesides, at an annual cost equal to four modestly priced tickets
for a single concert. But radio music, unless reproduced on a
super set, does not compare favourably with the actual presence
of an orchestra in the concert-hall. The sight of an artist or an
orchestra in action is conducive to attentive listening; for in the
case of the layman the eye aids the ear in assimilating the subtle-
ties of a score. Indeed, the actual presence of an orchestra is
essential to the new-comer to music, because the complicated
texture of the orchestration is at once made clear.

This may appear to the academic mind a strange way to
become accustomed to the initial difficulties of concentrated
listening, but I have discovered, and many other new-comers
too, that this is the most practical method. Whether the learned
gentlemen in their ivory towers agree or disagree, the fact remains that this is the method by which the new-comer often
gropes forward to the light. Unfortunately the new-comer is
apt to become experienced only in the ways of composers of the
past; the contemporary composers are usually completely unknown, unless one stumbles upon them by excellent good luck,
and not by fine judgment. My fortunate "finds" in these little-
performed compositions have been few and very far between.

During the last four years I have been attending concerts in
London two or three times weekly, and over that period of time
I have only heard Elgar's Violin Concerto once, which claimed

me as an admirer of this work at first hearing. During the same period I have heard violin concertos by foreign masters repeated time after time. It is to be expected, therefore, that when our own British composers are so neglected one should hear, as I once did, Vaughan Williams described as the chap who wrote "that *Greensleeves,* or something." The reason for such neglect was revealed to me by a chance meeting with a conductor through a friend of mine.

One of my social pleasures is meeting my friends at the local pub. Perhaps you may know that chance meetings, or introductions, with interesting people often happen in these places, especially if one of your drinking friends is a musical journalist. It was on one of these occasions that I met a well-known conductor who had recently returned from America. He gave an amusing account of how virtuoso conductors out there indulge in a little display of histrionics for the benefit of their almost swooning fans. This allowed me an opening—a very timid one in such a lions' den—to question him concerning the conductors in this country, and their attitude towards new or neglected works. His reply, in short, was that most conductors gave their "party pieces," which they conduct in preference to others.

This seems a hopeless setback for one keen on venturing as far as possible into the unknown realms of St. Cecilia. To find these sweet peregrinations arrested by those who should kindly lead us is frustration indeed. In fairness to the exceptions, I feel that, as a new-comer, I should like to hand a bouquet to Boyd Neel and his admirable little orchestra. The programmes he presents are varied and give one great opportunities to sample both classical and contemporary composers. One can attend the Boyd Neel concerts with confidence, without even viewing the prospects of the programme. I wish I had the same confidence in all concerts, especially solo recitals. The latter are among the biggest pitfalls of which the new-comer of limited means falls foul.

I was once attracted by a bill showing an elegantly-clad person in a pensive pose; but on attending the concert I witnessed a feeble male pianist tinkling through a programme of Chopin in a manner that by other yardsticks was a disgusting performance. On another occasion I heard a female, who called herself a dramatic soprano, screech and bawl like a Walt Disney animator burlesqueing operatic singing. On such occasions I have easily discerned the lack of quality in the performance. But it raised this doubt in my mind: how am I to know in my innocence (or ignorance) if I am obtaining the best value for my belated musical education, or if I am wasting my time listening to mediocre artists, thereby losing the finest pearls in my quest?

It should be the definite duty of the professional listener—the critic and musical journalist—to protect and guide us from this sort of thing. It is not good enough just to read in our dailies, perhaps the only reading matter we have time to glance through in these very busy days, that "Poltergeist" gave a brilliant performance, or the Bagwash Philharmonic Orchestra gave an indifferent interpretation of Kibbitzer's new symphony the previous night, if we new-comers did not attend the performances. I forbear with the journalist during these times of paper shortage, and know his allotted space is somewhat cramped, but I feel he could be more helpful to the concert-goer if he made use of his knowledge of past performances, and wrote on the possible merits, or demerits, of future performances.

I know it is impossible to give a preview of the capabilities of an artist or an orchestra appearing in this country for the first time. I would not expect even a music critic to achieve the impossible. He should consider it his task to guide the unwary to the righteous narrow path of finely performed concerts instead of allowing the poor wayfarer to wallow in bogs of declining tenors, and orchestras conducted by popular comedians.

The film fan or theatre patron has a fair chance to select his future entertainment, owing to the fact that film and theatre critics are given the opportunity to see the first of a series of performances of a new play or film, thereby giving the readers of their columns an idea of the entertainment value of current productions. A well-informed musical journalist should be able to forecast to some degree for his readers where, what, and why they should go to hear a particular performance. This helpful guide would assist a new-comer in saving time and money. Money in these matters is not of secondary importance to a great many concert-goers. The not-so-well-off can easily lose heart, and the musical world cannot afford to lose their enthusiastic support, because they represent the majority of the public.

The impecunious music-lover may not be academic, his ignorance may or may not be deep, but what are we to think of a journalist like Gordon Glover, who reiterates a well-known comedian's quip in describing Charlie Shadwell as "the poor man's Adrian Boult"? Sir Adrian Boult might earn a better living conducting a bus if he were totally dependent upon the rich for his followers. This kind of remark reminds me of the débutante who, on becoming aware of one of the natural human functions, enquired if the poor people were similarly endowed. When she was told that this was so, she replied that it was "far too good for them."

Gordon Glover is not the only offender to lower the dignity of musical journalism. It seems, for instance, that Mr. Whittaker of the *Evening Standard* rarely offers in his columns any evidence of conclusions drawn by himself. Again, the *Daily Express* boasts of its large circulation, but its efforts to create a useful or informative column for its readers with musical interests are lamentable. It is not good enough to read that a certain eminent pianist changed her name by adopting her mother's maiden name, or to read what grandpapa called a great violinist when he was a little boy. A musical journalist should have better use for his space than to imitate the cheap blurb that is applied to the doings of popular film stars who appear to have nothing more to recommend them than their appearance in the latest fashion in sweaters!

There are others whose didactic writing would lose quite a lot of its length and grandeur if they refrained from quoting from the

THE ORCHESTRA LOOKS
AT THE AUDIENCE

Frederick Thurston

*

IF you sat in the orchestra, you would have a very different view of music-making. To us, audiences are a sea of faces and moving programmes. While we wait for the conductor to appear, our time is occupied with looking for faces we know, seeing that we are not in a cramped position for playing, and doing a little quiet tuning. If there is a new work on the programme, perhaps we glance at the seats where we know the leading critics are sitting, and wonder what they are going to say about it, and on very rare occasions we see they have gone out, before the end, then we *know* what they are thinking. You applaud the conductor or the soloist when he comes on: your clapping hands moving in rhythm. We wonder if you are clapping the man as a musician, as an interpreter of the works you have come to hear, or whether it is just his personality which carries you away.

At the end of a performance, our trained ears detect a perfunctory, formal note in the clapping for the overture; the hysterical last-night-of-the-proms stamping and banging, for the soloist—if he is a well-known virtuoso; and the genuine slow-to-start and then *crescendo* applause that means you are really satisfied with the symphony.

Often you are wrong in the applause you have given—or we think you are. We know when (by that miracle of perfection which so seldom happens) we have worked together for once as an immaculate team under a conductor at once masterful, erudite, and yet sympathetic. Yet when this happens the applause is frequently no greater, even if as great, as on many mediocre occasions. Again, there are times, as with every team, when slight disharmonies—perhaps due to over-tiredness, an unsympathetic conductor, a new work insufficiently rehearsed, or a familiar work played to death—when we feel that the performance was distinctly below our best, but the applause will seldom reflect our own self-criticism.

Why is this? There may be two reasons. First, in the mass you may not be sufficiently discriminating to be able to appreciate all that goes to make the perfect performance. Perhaps some of you may be a little uncertain as to whether it is good or bad, and will be carried away by the first man who starts off with a hearty clap to follow automatically, and by herd instinct, the lead he has given. Alternatively, it may be that if the general level of applause is feeble, your individual vigorous response does not reach us on the platform. I have heard a member of an audience shout out, "Thank God that's over" after a performance of a new work in the Queen's Hall, but of course that needs a certain kind of courage.

The second reason may be that we ourselves may have reached a wrong judgment, for the simple reason that we can never hear the proper effect of our own playing. We are too near the wood to hear the trees. The full ensemble is only heard at some distance from the orchestra. In my seat, for instance, I am—in some concert-halls—20 or 25 feet from the nearest 'cello, and only 6 or 8 feet from the four horn players. In a *tutti* passage, played fortissimo, I am bound to hear the brass to the almost total exclusion of the 'cellos, and indeed most of the strings. Therefore, although we can tell defects of intonation and ensemble in passage work, we can seldom hear what *you* hear in the matter of the all-important balance.

We look at you, when all the seats are taken and you are an enthusiastic audience, and try to guess what has brought you all in. Is it the conductor, the soloist, the programme? We know that Beethoven, Brahms, and Tchaikovsky will always attract you. Does the weather have much to do with your attendance?—

I mean, on a lovely evening do you decide to take the air, and leave us to stifle by ourselves in the hall? And if it's wet, do you stop at home for *that* reason?

We cannot tell what your emotions are, and, of course, neither can you tell how we feel, which is perhaps as well. On one occasion our Principal Flute arrived for the concert, having just received a cheque for £600. He treated everybody to a drink in the staff bar, and played the concert feeling on top of the world.

I remember also when in Bedford, one of the war-time bases of the B.B.C. Symphony Orchestra, we had, only a few days after arriving in the town, rehearsed in a distant studio. I met the conductor over an early dinner between the rehearsal and the performance; and while we dined, the fog came down thick and heavy. Leaving it perhaps a little late, I got into my car with the conductor, and in a few moments we were completely lost. One of the many visitors to the town kindly directed us up the wrong street. The minutes were flying. We knew the red light would be flickering, and a considerable audience in the studio sitting in their places. Both the conductor and I, as you can well imagine, were in a state of tense anxiety, and yet I had to drive with the utmost care in the thick fog.

The minutes went by; five minutes to go; four minutes to go; turn left; no, turn right; up here; along there; down this way, until eventually, when the performance must have been either abandoned or well under way, we arrived at the studio. The leader, Paul Beard, had started conducting the concert, and at the end of the first movement of the first work he quietly slipped back into his place, the conductor took up his baton, and unobtrusively I slipped into my seat. The audience in the studio may perhaps have wondered at this, but they heard the music just the same. The millions of listeners over the air knew nothing of the happening at all, but in the whole of my life I have seldom been so anxious as during those ten minutes in the fog.

Are some of you in the audience really bored and indifferent when you come to a concert-hall? Do you come merely because it is "the thing to do," because it is raining outside, or because you have nowhere else to go? If you are, you are in a mood roughly corresponding with that experienced sometimes by some of us orchestral players when we are just earning our living by playing a dull pot-boiler programme under an indifferent conductor, playing a new work we feel instinctively to be worthless, or maybe we are completely jaded, with our interest in any music at the ultimate ebb. Are you sometimes very thrilled at the emotional experience you hope for? Are you highly strung, ready to be swayed by the music? You do not often betray any of these feelings if you have them.

But, on the other hand, perhaps we do not let you see our occasional show of nerves at an awkward passage written by a composer, who was not aware of the peculiar difficulties of the instrument in that register. Some of us naturally are more sensitive than others. We may be in a state of extreme tension—not only because of an unfortunate experience before the concert, or toothache which makes us wonder if we can do our best—but because we know that our professional career depends on as faultless a performance as possible *every* time.

One can get away with a "domino" once—even twice, but then someone starts to say: "Poor Blank, he is beginning to slip, he isn't what he was." String players may fear a passage which, if the conductor takes it a shade too fast, is unplayable; or they may be nervous about the heat of the room affecting their tuning. This factor applies in even greater measure to us of the wood-wind, because the limits of adjustment we may make are very small. We worry sometimes about moisture clogging the pads of the keys of our instruments, and our section of the orchestra has perhaps the greatest cause of possible disaster inherent in the design of the instrument—our reeds. A good reed is so rare that we are frequently using reeds we do not *quite* trust; and when the vital solo passages, with which we are so often confronted, are just over the page, there is sometimes the terrible thought that the reed may let us down. I doubt if members of an audience have any musical cause to suffer emotionally like that, although I have heard people say that when an extremely sensitive passage is about to be played, and they fear the worst, they must close their ears so that, good or bad, they do not hear it.

The brass players, as well as ourselves, have constant thoughts that the vital, sensitive, and delicate lip muscles may be off colour, with the result that distress and anxiety are caused when an instrument has to stand out above the orchestra. The harpist knows the fear of snapping strings; the tympanist the anxiety caused by a thoughtless composer, who asks for an enormous change of pitch of his instruments in a period of time too short for it to be accomplished without the most breathless rush.

I do not want you to think that our life is all anxiety. There are many, many times when, even if we do not reach the ultimate heights of performance, we are able to feel satisfied that we have given a fair interpretation of the composer's intentions; and that, individually, we have acquitted ourselves well.

We may, perhaps, irritate you by failing to play a work exactly as you think we ought: *you* have several ways of irritating us. At the Proms a group of young students often gather as close to the orchestra as possible, and with open scores, which they flap over with self-conscious care, they nudge each other with meaning winks as they detect some slight deviation from the printed copy. This deviation was made perhaps at rehearsal, after much care and thought, by the conductor in collaboration with the players most affected. Then you may cough in the *pianissimo* passages; you insist on recall after recall for a soloist, to the detriment of the timing of the programme, and a consequent missing of 'buses and trains by many of us. You sometimes fail to come in reasonable numbers to hear an important new work, or a revival of a rarely heard masterpiece, to the rehearsal of which we have devoted infinite care and much more time than usual. You can make foolish remarks in the bars during the interval about a work which we know has taken months and months of the concentrated effort of a serious composer, and dismiss it as "rubbish" on the first hearing, without studying the score or having the slightest knowledge of his intentions. You can lavish adulation on a conductor whom we know to be 90 per cent. personality and 10 per cent. musician. You can say *his* Beethoven surpasses all, whereas we know that what matters is Beethoven, and that if Mr. X has given the great master the benefit of his personal interpretation, he has committed as great an artistic flaw as you have in wrongly allotting your praise.

When we look out beyond the bright lights of the platform, we can seldom see *you* as individuals: we tend to think of you as a mass, which of course you are not. You tend to think of *us* as individuals (especially, of course, the principals).

There, of course, you are only partially right. We are first and foremost a team, in which each individual must subjugate his personality to the whole. I think it only fair to my colleagues to say that there seems to me no other form of team work in industry, art, or sport, in which one man depends so much on the other as in orchestral playing. Each individual's contribution is closely knit with that of his colleagues, and there is a common zealousness for success of the whole combined effort of the hundred players on the platform. This, I think, must be unique among all those occupations in which men join together for a common task.

Finally, your attendance at concerts gives us our daily bread; without you, concerts would never happen. And without us Beethoven, Brahms, and Stravinsky would never come to life for you.

STANDARDS OF PERFORMANCE

Geoffrey   Sharp

*

TEN years ago, when life was more civilised than it is to-day, a fair standard of performance, whether in theatre or concert-hall, could be taken for granted; while performances of the highest class were sufficiently frequent to goad and spur those "artists" with little conscience and less ability (of whom we have always had plenty) to play, sing, or act a little better than they, or we, thought they could.

This is not the time or the place to clean the theatrical sink, which would be a Herculean labour, but we may perhaps try to let some daylight into the money-grubbing gloom that threatens to eliminate artistry altogether from the business of concert-promoting.

Cast your mind back—and your imagination—if you will, to the concerts of 1938. The Vienna Philharmonic under Bruno Walter, the Berlin Philharmonic under Furtwängler, the London Philharmonic under Beecham: these three combinations set an orchestral standard which others tried to imitate with varying success. The first two were war casualties so far as we in this country are concerned, while the third partnership has become a very vague shadow of the miracle it used to be at its best.

As compensation, London is afflicted with a superabundance of indifferent orchestras of mushroom growth, a resurgence of the old evil known as the deputy system and a concentration on the ballet, presumably in the hope that the large, new, uneducated public will be so distracted by the dancing that they will not notice the poverty of the playing. In fact, there is something so rotten about London's orchestral music that it stinks. Three rays of hope, however, are beginning to pierce the fog: the new Royal Philharmonic Orchestra which Sir Thomas Beecham launched at Croydon in September, the recent very great improvement of the London Philharmonic (notably under Victor de Sabata), and the promise shown by the Covent Garden Orchestra which played particularly well for Franco Capuana and had the astonishing temerity to sack players who sent deputies!

It would be possible, though not easy, to set matters right. London could support three symphony orchestras run on a basis of all-round integrity, implying fair conditions for hard work and a good standard of pay. Wages, though, should not be excessive: high pay does not ensure a corresponding artistic standard, but usually begets only greed, idleness, and conceit, the three most paralysing symptoms of artistic nullity—all of them prevalent among British orchestral musicians to-day.

Three full symphony orchestras, each of 120 players, would of course entail three first-class permanent conductors; they would also require three, or at the very least two, adequate concert-halls, of which there is not one in London to-day, and they would have to enrol 360 first-class musicians all prepared to put first things first—there are still some of these, but not many.

We should be less polemical if there were any sign of a move being made in the right direction; but there isn't. Chappell & Co. are not rebuilding Queen's Hall on account of obstruction and red tape, while Manchester's Free Trade Hall also remains a shell which only a brave Whitehall apologist dare excuse by claiming that the Government are too busy not building houses to bother with concert-halls.

The United States, which it would be unwise to imitate too slavishly, at least manage some of their affairs well, particularly those which we manage worst. They have welcomed from the continent of Europe, and from these islands, countless artists whom they have absorbed into their vast community to the advantage of all concerned; while we have been and are almost exclusively occupied with local boys and girls, of great talent and none, with the result that our range of vision still stretches little beyond the parish pump.

Consider the problem of orchestral conductors. Those of the first rank are, and will always remain, few and far between. The war years have aggravated the position by taking from us Greenbaum, Harty, Heward, Weingartner, and Wood: yet Ansermet, van Beinum, Dobrowen, Sabata, and Wolff have all visited this country during the last few months to be given a tepid and often vacillating reception by the British press, whose music criticism a foreign visitor has described as the least venomous but also the silliest in the civilised world. We have to admit that it is seldom venomous and very often stupid. Consider, for example, Menuhin's recent performance of the Elgar Concerto at the Proms; his intonation was lamentable for an artist of international repute, there was no consistency of style in his interpretation and little evidence of logical cohesion in the musical argument he presented. Now all of these are points in which Menuhin has formerly excelled. Why didn't the musical press as a whole descend upon him like an avalanche instead of merely one or two bold spirits with integrity enough to sour the soothing syrup of general sycophantic praise? Reflect also, if you will, on the time it has taken our critics to acclaim the genius of Victor de Sabata: newspaper criticism must form the vanguard of public opinion, away with the old fogies who instinctively prefer to travel in the guard's van. Let us encourage the impetuous critic, even if, on occasion, he chooses to give Barbirolli a lesson in conducting—the one first-class conductor in England fully occupied in a position which gives him scope for his great abilities as an orchestral trainer.

Then we must not forget Sir Thomas Beecham, whose periodic oscillations from one side of the Atlantic to the other have so far prevented him from re-establishing his position in this country as one to whom all others turn for a lesson in musical perfection—and such lessons are at a premium just now. Many others "also run," but we are not particularly interested to see them finish the course: we believe it is Beecham, Barbirolli *et praeterea nihil* in Great Britain in 1946. What of the future?

You may remember that some months ago Wilhelm Furt-wängler was for all practical purposes a "displaced person," without an orchestra or any immediate prospect of a job and obviously ready to consider any genuine offer that might be made having due regard to his earlier attainments and prestige. There was a rumour that he would come to England to conduct the National Symphony Orchestra: what he would have thought of this miscellaneous body is beside the point, for we must not forget that this man is a German, nay worse, a Prussian, who held a position as Staatsrat under the Nazi *régime,* and therefore, of course, it would not have been desirable for him to come to this country and corrupt our people's politics—or perhaps debunk our amateurish music-making with a salutary dose of the real thing which we have almost forgotten.

It is clear what should have been done and we are not being wise after the event, having put forward this suggestion while there was still time for it to be adopted: Furtwängler should have been offered the permanent conductorship of one of our less inferior orchestras with *carte blanche* to dismiss and engage per-sonnel and establish conditions of rehearsal, in the same way as Bruno Walter should have been engaged for the Hallé Orchestra years ago. Once again we have missed the bus: Neville Cham-berlain was an excellently representative prime minister for this country—we are always missing the bus.

Probably at this point, if not before, readers will begin to demur about the war and the admittedly difficult conditions which it incurred. Quite so, but the war is over, however rare the signs; yet the Concertgebouw Orchestra of Amsterdam is as fine as ever it was, and only the most bigoted partisan could pretend that conditions in Holland were less rigorous than here.

Adequate rehearsal is the lynch-pin of the whole problem.

Yet it is a truism that the rank and file of British conductors, having "run through" their programme once in rehearsal, can think of nothing further to do! It is manifestly useless to offer such men facilities on a level with (for example) Furtwängler, for orchestra and conductor would then make a precipitous descent even further into the yawning chasm of boredom and ineptitude than has been plumbed already. It is not true that there are no bad orchestras—merely bad conductors; but John Barbirolli with the Hallé and Victor de Sabata with the London Philharmonic have shown very clearly how a conductor of genius can literally work wonders with an orchestra which previously had been playing to a very mediocre standard. Though such wonders are likely to be prejudiced by the recent decree of the Musicians' Union raising the fees for all rehearsals extra to the first.

To be logical, which is seldom among an artist's strongest features, we should first plan and build (not plan and shelve) a series of satisfactory concert-halls. Neither London nor Manchester has one, for their respective Alberts are inadequate for a variety of reasons, and only dire necessity could drive a symphony orchestra into a circus ring.

The Henry Wood Memorial Hall will fill an urgent need, if it is ever built. The ideal concert-hall should seat between 3,000 and 4,000: London's Albert Hall is too big, apart from its shocking acoustics, while in a hall seating less than 3,000 it is difficult if not impossible to run a concert season on an economic basis. We agree with the late Sir Henry Wood that music must not be asked to pay, but unfortunately no nation of shopkeepers can be expected to understand this, and commercial instincts will no doubt continue to run deeper than artistic in the bone of most of us. Certainly this is true of the majority of orchestral players who have shown, during the war years, a disconcerting avarice for gold (or what now passes as a substitute) and have therefore in many cases turned their attention to the films as being more lucrative and in general less strenuous than proper music-making.

The past six years have given additional proof, if it were needed, that in time of war, when mankind is obsessed with brutalities to a degree not challenged by the beasts, our devotion to the arts, which appeared so strong in peace, becomes but a thin veneer. In music, which is all that concerns us here, standards are sacrificed to expediency. They have been, and we are now paying the price. The moral is too obvious to point. We need a change of heart: musicians must try to imagine the chaos that would ensue before they demand higher and ever higher wages for rehearsal and performance. They must, of course, be paid a respectable living wage, but if they insist on profiteering by the lack of taste, experience, and understanding which is written large across the faces of present-day audiences, then orchestral music in this country will remain what it has generally become: artless, in the literal sense.

We do not urge Government control; that would be fatal and finally so. There can be no reincarnation of any art which has once been stifled by bureaucrats. But the Government could do far more to help than they have done so far. We should like to see a reasonable settlement of the problem of Queen's Hall, not in the remote future but *now*. Then we should like to see a complete remission of Entertainment Tax on all concerts which can be shown to have a genuine educational value. It is a mere quibble to oppose such a plan on the ground that no two people would agree on what is and what is not educational. By derivation the term "education" is a very broad one, let the Government be generous and put a broad interpretation on it.

To sum up: music is a microcosm of life. Any other definition must be incomplete. Scientists, philosophers, theologians, and even politicians have been at pains to tell us in recent months that what we need is a new approach: an era of goodwill, not merely passive but militant goodwill, ready and eager to work for the development of a higher and more wholesome attitude towards all that is most worthwhile, by which we mean intrinsically rewarding. Music rewards us exactly in proportion to the effort we make on its behalf. Nobody ever got anything for nothing out of art.

Let us then put our house in order and aim consistently at perfection as we understand it. We are not likely often to achieve our aim, but a close approximation carefully prepared will always earn a measure of sympathetic appreciation, while the shoddy, commonplace, commercial travesty contributes only to the ultimate discredit and degradation of orchestral music, which in its turn will drive our orchestral musicans through a series of jobs unworthy of their attainments until they emerge, cap in hand, on the streets of our industrial cities. That their swift decline will be largely their own fault should not prevent us doing all we can to prevent it.

TO START AN ARGUMENT

I : What is the Purpose of Music?

★

SCOTT GODDARD SAYS—

THE purpose of music is the purpose of those who come in contact with music, the uses to which they put it either as creative artist, interpretative artist, or listener. It is the last that interests me at the moment. The purpose of the creative artist, the composer, may be self-expression or the urge to better mankind. That of the executant may also be self-expression or the need to make a living. The purpose of the listener may be to use music as a background noise, which for him becomes the purpose of music while he becomes not a listener but a hearer. Or it may be to use music for widening his apprehension of intellectual values. It is with this latter type that I shall deal here. I consider him the more valuable since, having ceased merely to hear and having begun to listen, he has begun to curb his rawer emotions and to approach music in a spirit of inquiry. His is the wondering mind of the student. He is to discover the essence of music so that he may in time recognise its effects and use it to the best purpose, as an adjunct, that is, to the production of the complete man.

The purpose of music for my Ideal Listener is to increase awareness of the phenomena of existence. He will not allow music to take him places until he discovers which places precisely he is being taken to and what they have to offer. The "heights" to which music is supposed to raise mankind have never been surveyed, only viewed from a distance through the bleared eyes of emotion; nor have the "depths" been explored with the slightest degree of accuracy. To be accurate in assessing the various values of music is not fashionable. It is as though we were afraid that by inquiring into the differing purposes demanded of music we should forfeit the emotion it so powerfully provides: the heat about the heart, the associations ("Darling, didn't that remind you of . . . ?") and the swooning ecstasy of the addict. Probably we should lose there. And a cruel loss it would be were there nothing with which to fill the void. That is part of the popular fear of allowing that our purpose with music might place it on any other level than that of emotion. We are afraid lest by approaching music through our intelligence we shall lose the ability to use music for stimulating our most cherished emotions. The argument is, however, not consecutive; for the intelligent use of music does not of necessity exclude its use for the purpose of emotional stimulation. The return road is still open. Only then the return will be made deliberately, the listener choosing the emotional approach instead of being chosen by it. It is improbable that this type of listener, having enjoyed that other stimulus of the intellect, will want to use music for exciting the lower nerve centres, unless to experiment with them or with music. But if he so desire, he can take that road again.

Music will give any answer that is desired of it, according as it is used for purposes of entertainment (domestic background noise), as a spur to action (the recruiting sergeant's band), as pure excitation (aphrodisiac, soporific), as an aid to meditation (a rare and dangerous use of sound to produce certain states of spiritual exaltation), none of these needing knowledge of music itself or therefore demanding study of music as an art. On the other hand, my Ideal Listener does desire to know and will be impelled to study. And that is another reason why the emotionalist fears what he calls the highbrow, by which he means the person who refuses blindly to accept and wants to know what he is being sold and what effect it will have on him. "Are audiences," people ask, "now to be expected to show intelligence about music?" For all time, as far as we can tell, music has been used for the purpose of caressing us like a warm bath, exciting us like alcohol, giving us dreams like mescal. What is the good of pretending that we in the audience will enjoy it any more if we study it? There's enough to study as it is. Leave us our relaxation." It is odd that this plea to be left alone should have been fostered not only by purveyors of entertainment but often by performers. Did they fear that their province would be invaded? They need not have done so. Those who study to become intelligent listeners have another purpose than to become public performers. Their education in listening will not lead them to the concert platform.

Whoever sees this purpose in the treatment of music will indeed feel the need for education. And so the question becomes one of the appreciation of music. Musical Appreciation is a term that came into prominence during the first quarter of the century, was overdone and often wrongly applied, so that eventually within the last ten years it has come into disrepute. There are nevertheless signs that the importance of a right appreciation is no less conceded now than before; thus the term is coming into use once again and being employed with less diffidence. It is, indeed, this idea of the right appreciation of music that is at the centre of the question of music's place in the life of man. We may take it, I think, that the aim of this ideal education is the production of good people. Whether they be looked on as citizens of a city, or of a state, or ideally as citizens of the world, they must be, in the most enlightened estimate, complete persons, men and women in control of themselves, and thus able to direct and educate the generations entrusted to them. They must be in no way at the mercy of their passions when making decisions for themselves or others. By their education they must be able to escape from the sway of artificially propagated emotional stimuli. They must, in fact, know what they are hearing in prose, in verse, in musical sound as easily and inevitably as they know what they are looking at in buildings, sculpture, and painting. They must cease to be hearers and become listeners. They must discriminate among the various manifestations of art that surround them; and adequately to do that they will need to undertake training in the ancillary art of appreciation.

The aim in training intelligent listeners is to foster a complete understanding of the materia musica by acute listening; and so highly to cultivate memory that the listener will be able to compass the task. It is much more exacting than any undertaken by the gazer at pictures or the reader, who can always turn back to recapture a lost clue; the task, I mean, of following the processes of thought in music logically and consecutively, even when the material in which that thought is expressed has no lasting power and is as evanescent as sound, for it is but sound.

This training will do more than enhance pleasure; it will increase man's power over his environment. And should it be suggested that this is a strange claim to make for the most emotional of all the arts, the reply is that music in itself is not mere emotion. We have too long allowed only that, more hindrance than help, to reach us from music. The fault lies with us, and with us, too, the remedy. It is to cease to treat music as one of the frivolous decorations of life, one of the social opportunities, as we treat a good dinner-party or the food we provide for such an event. If we treat music in that way, it will retaliate as food and drink do when heedlessly taken into our systems while we are not watching but doing something else. There is no excuse for us who have a million masterpieces of consecutive and logical thought upon which we may expend our abilities as thinkers, not feelers.

"Music that brings sweet sleep down from the blissful skies." In the lotus-land of perpetual afternoon-tea there is a place reserved for Orsino. There he sits, close up against the grand piano, murmuring ceaselessly, "That strain again." He will never know any more. The one tune has sufficiently stirred his emotions, and that is all he has allowed music to do. For him that alone is the Purpose of Music. Music while you work: "Fetch me my knitting, dear, while I listen to the wireless."

On the Other Hand

*

C. B. REES SAYS—

It is not my intention in this article to enunciate a philosophy or an ethic, or to give an objective summary of other people's views. I shall be completely personal, subjective, and unashamed, writing as one who loves and enjoys music. Until the Editor asked me for this article, I had never, I confess, seriously thought about the "purpose" of music. How many of you have?

I admit that, as a youngster—then indifferent to music, and with few facilities for listening to it anyway—I had imbibed a notion that music is "uplifting"; that, somehow, it did "good"; that it had a moral end. I vividly remember being taken to "sacred" concerts; I remember announcements in chapel about forthcoming performances of "sacred" music. And I remember noticing that whereas weekday music-making used to be billed as "concert" or "grand concert" (especially "grand"), such occasions on Sundays were always described as "sacred." So, you see, it was not difficult for me to acquire a belief that there was an essential connection between religion, ethics, morality (call it what you will) and music—the best music. Performances of *Messiah, Elijah*, the stock oratorios of my early recollections, were not so much musical as religious events. I had to put on my best suit for these, and be on my best behaviour. . . .

I used to think that musicians were necessarily rather "better" people than others, that they were of finer fibre, especially if they specialised in oratorio. But, later, I discovered, as part of that bracing disillusionment which is called education, that my early acquired and unexamined assumptions were not true, were not even sensible. I got to know musicians of all kinds, and discovered that they are just as "human" as actors, sailors, bootblacks, or even journalists: often more so. They do not appear to have been necessarily improved as men and women

OPERA

Sadler's Wells Opera production of Vaughan Williams's
"Sir John in Love" at Sadler's Wells Theatre

The Immortal Falstaff—The Merry Wives of Windsor

The Boar Inn, a pub of low character which was typical
of this isolated part of Suffolk in the 18th century

Sadler's Wells Opera production of Benjamin Britten's
"Peter Grimes" at Sadler's Wells Theatre

Peter returns after three days alone at
sea, hungry, wet, frenzied, almost insane

Luigi declares his love for Giogetta, wife of Michele

Giogetta and
Michele remem-
ber the days
of their early
love when he
sheltered her
under his cloak

Sadler's Wells Opera pro
of Puccini's "Il Tabarro"
at Sadler's Wells Theatre

he plan in action. Guglielmo and Ferrando testing the fidelity of their sweethearts

add to my 'bid' another
y, if you'll join in the plan.
ou agree?"

's Wells Opera production
ozart's "Cosi fan Tutte"
adler's Wells Theatre

BALLET

Sadler's Wells Ballet production of "Symphonic Variations" at the Royal Opera House, Covent Garden

This ballet has no story to it. It is a virtuoso piece for six virtuoso dancers, an interpretation in terms of pure dancing of César Franck's famous composition for piano and orchestra

Four princes seek the Princess Aurora's hand in marriage

Prince Charming
woos the vision
of the lovely
Princess Aurora

er's Wells Ballet
uction of "The
ping Princess" at the
al Opera House,
ent Garden

Sadler's Wells Ballet production of "*Adam Zero*"
at the Royal Opera House, Covent Garden

"Adam Zero" symbolises Man's progress and disintegration from birth to death. The process is depicted by means of a ballet within a ballet, and skilled use is made of every stage device shattering the illusion that ballet has built up

PERSONALITIES

Sir Thomas Beecham in action

ARTUR SCHNABEL, the American pianist of Austrian origin

GREGOR FITELBERG in action

(*right*) VICTOR DE SABATA in repose

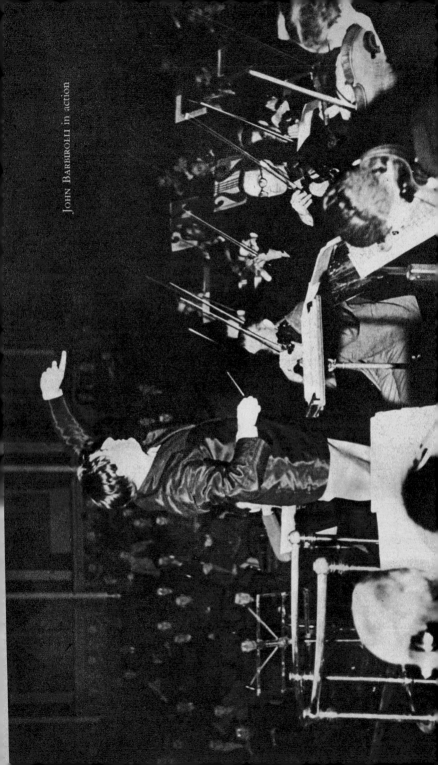
John Barbirolli in action

by their experiences as artists. Music has not made them "good";
at least not any better than they were *au fond*.

My subsequent years of ardent, constant concert-going and
wireless listening have induced in me now the conviction that
music has no "purpose" at all. It is not intended to make a better
world. It is not meant to make bad men good and good men
better. It has nothing to offer a distracted democracy or a defeated
oligarchy in the way of solutions to current problems. True, it
may make you forget a toothache—so will a sharp attack of
lumbago. It may give you a feeling of exaltation—so will good
wine. It may soothe harassed and jangled nerves—so will any
reliable soporific.

We are too ready in this country to associate music with
morality. Think of the endless denunciations of jazz as "immoral."
Heaven knows, I hate jazz (I don't like its noises as noises), but
I cannot believe it to be more immoral than skating. Some of
the hymns sung in our churches are more offensive, musically,
however unexceptionable the sentiments they may express.
Music is an art (and science, too). It exists for its own sake. The
fact that *Tristan* may make you feel erotic and Beethoven's Ninth
Symphony make you feel spiritually elevated does not make
Wagner's music erotic or Beethoven's morally reformative.

In the philosophical sense, therefore, I submit that there is no
purpose to music; that it is not "for" anything; that it is not a
useful instrument for the fabrication of saints. Beethoven's
Fifth Symphony may be Fate—or Kate—knocking at the door.
That is up to you. But if you look at the score you will see that
the first movement is marked *allegro con brio*. That is not up to
you. It is a business, a highly important business, between Beethoven and the orchestra and conductor.

Of course, the artist, especially the great creative artist, works
under æsthetic and personal compulsions of which we may know
little, and about which little that is really enlightening may be
deduced from his work. The impulses and processes of creation
are obscurely hidden; they vary in different men; they vary from

M.M. 1—3

time to time in the same man. But even when a composer writes a work to explain, or at any rate express, his relationship to God, or man's place and significance (or insignificance) in the cosmos, it does not follow that it is the intention and design of music as an art to do so. In the novels of Dickens there are powerful exposures of contemporary social evils, but it is not the purpose of the novel to expose social evil, although, of course, it may do so (and often does) with tremendous salutary effect.

The love of music, also, appears to exist for its own sake. In my listening I am not conscious of purpose, in the sense that I am when I climb a hill in order to get to the village on the other side of it, or when I take up a difficult book, say, on some aspect of economics, and sweat over it in order to try to understand the theory of rent or the distribution of the national income. In his *A Key to the Art of Music* Frank Howes has a pertinent paragraph to this effect:

". . . This disinterested quality, this absence of all purpose beyond itself is an essential characteristic of all art, and of music even more than the others which occasionally are involved in doing a useful piece of work, as when a sculptor commemorates a battle or a general, and a painter illustrates a book or designs a carpet . . ."

Our own individual attitude to music has a close connection with, and is conditioned by, our views as to its purpose (or purposelessness). I go to a concert for "pleasure." Do you? I want to hear Mozart or Handel or Dvořák; I am interested in conductor X or Y, in how he will do this or that; I am anxious to get to know better this or that concerto (there is a limited purpose here, but purely subjective).

In other words, music becomes Entertainment. In this country we do not sufficiently regard it in that light. The heavy frown of the Puritan still commands in us a self-conscious, if more reluctant, attention. Our concert-halls (when we have any) are usually fashioned more in the style of mausoleums than as "halls of song." We must be disciplined by discomfort into a proper appreciation of great art. We must not smoke. It is better that we should look solemn. On no account must we express disapproval, certainly not by hissing; and our applause must be polite, gentlemanly, not violent enough to make the people in front turn round with mute disapproval. Refreshments must be difficult to obtain, not too good in quality, harboured in dark and dismal bars. Programme notes must be dutifully academic, making sure that the "second subject is ushered in by the woodwind . . ." Performances, too, had better be on the sedate side. No crude vitality, *if* you please! And *any* foreigner must, of course, be "*quite* superb." How can a man with a name like Smith compare with a man with a name like Spoziglob? The times of concerts should, naturally, conform with our social customs and eating habits, so that nobody shall be compelled to stay out late, nobody shall be denied the opportunity to use the concert-period for the leisured digestion of a meal and the surreptitious snatching of forty winks during the "dull part" of the slow movement. Preferably, if an arrangement can be made with the authorities, all public-houses in the vicinity of the music-making should close early (or not open at all) to avoid the spread of the pernicious Continental habit of meeting after the music to discuss it—and DRINKING.

Enjoyment, did you say? Really! What would the professors, the pedants, the solemn academicians think? What about the atmosphere of the lecture-hall, the classroom, the humid study, the hushed examination-room? No vulgarity! You would think, to hear some people talk, that music was like a good meal, or a vintage wine. T'ch, t'ch! Where is the exercise of the intellect, where the sublimation of the crude senses, where the elevated and elevating spirituality? Where, indeed?

But, surely, music is to be enjoyed precisely like fine cooking, or a vintage wine, or a lovely sunset (what is *that* for?), or a sonnet by Shakespeare, or a rolling, tossing sea viewed from a headland.

A vast new public for music multiplies the responsibilities of those who cater for it. Why give that public hair-shirts? Let us abolish the sense of sin and substitute a sense of sun. Let us enjoy our music uninhibited, take it for what it is, for itself, in itself, by itself.

I remember some years ago after a thrilling performance by Toscanini of a Wagner programme, meeting a musical friend just beyond the steps of the Queen's Hall. He felt as excited as I did, and said to me: "Heavens, that's how music should sound. I could go off and kiss a policeman. . . ."

No, he was not an impressionable youth, not an uninformed enthusiast who deals always in superlatives. He was a scholarly, critical, sceptical-minded individual. I have often thought of his spontaneous and rather comic indication of his reaction to that concert. One does not often come away from a concert feeling like that. After many of them I feel more like heaving a brick at a policeman—or at somebody less innocent of responsibility for the defects of the occasion. Don't let us be highbrowed into solemnity, into turning artistic fun into a religious rite. We should take our music as naturally as we take a glass of beer with a friend. What is the "purpose" of our beer and our conversation? What is the "purpose" of our appreciation of a beautiful woman? I have no idea.

I am equally bereft of ideas about the purpose of music—unless it is to send us off to kiss a policeman.

PERSONALITY CORNER

C. B. Rees

★

No matter what criticisms are levelled against the "cult" of personalities, whether in art, literature, or politics, it remains generally true that "oomph" (or its equivalent) will capture interest and attention to which homespun merit, self-disregarding sincerity, and plain devotion beckon in vain. This is as evident (if not more so) in the concert-hall as anywhere else.

Much of the interest that centres on concert-giving is due to this fact, not to preoccupation with the abstractions of music. How good or bad this may be I am not concerned to estimate. I merely observe the fact, and in recent weeks in London there have been many opportunities to encounter some striking personalities, and, for those interested in the study, to watch their impact on audiences—and performers, yes, and on music too. But it is with the personalities, as such, that we shall linger.

I confess that I knew very little about VICTOR DE SABATA, and had never previously seen him, when I was urged to attend some of his concerts in London with the London Philharmonic Orchestra. He limped energetically on to the rostum, turned a pale rather grim face to the audience, and then, in a few seconds, exploded into an astonishing paroxysm of postures—leaping, heaving, dancing, boxing, crouching, waving, and at any moment apparently about to take off into the roof.

The eye of the beholder was so startled at first that the ear forgot to function. A man sitting next to me laughed, not too softly for good behaviour. I looked at Sabata again. He was still there, his bald head shining, his fringe of white hair making more incongruous his incredible athleticism. But I still couldn't quite believe it. "Clowning," a friend called it—in the first few minutes of the overture. Only in the first few minutes.

One heard the music. The eye ignored the spectacle as the ear grew to delight in the sound. The man who had laughed turned round and bent his head sharply in a knowing gesture of approbation. And at the close of the work the audience loudly shouted its spontaneous tribute. We have often said that it does not matter if a conductor stands on his head so long as he produces good results. But I personally had never before come across a conductor who very nearly did stand on his head—and produced magnificent results.

When I met this remarkable Italian maestro, I found that off the rostrum he had a monumental calm, so long as he had his shabby soft hat on his head to keep off the refrigerating draughts of the early English summer. He looked to me very much like the picture of Julius Cæsar that adorned the De Bello Gallico of my schooldays. Quick and fiery at rehearsal, carrying all the music in his finely shaped head, he seemed to turn off the combustion in social contact. His measured manner and slow smile and genial ease contrasted sharply with his incandescence on the job.

There may be, indeed there are, differences of opinion about his interpretations, but there can be none about his rocket-like impact on the orchestras he conducts. They enjoy it—even if they have to.

John Barbirolli has also been delighting our musical occasions, and showing Londoners that there is no need to be a "foreigner" in order to be artistically good. He keeps his feet firmly planted on the rostrum and his gestures within the bounds of the normal geometric world, but lets his temperament and imagination soar.

To see this short, taut, dark figure come briskly to the platform is to have one's attention riveted at once. He is already intent on his destination—the best possible performance—from which nothing will deflect him. Discipline, but not unsmiling, is written in his very stance. Oh, yes, he will drive the orchestra and the chorus too. I watched him rehearse the B.B.C. Symphony Orchestra and the B.B.C. Choral Society for Verdi's *Requiem*. No flagging, least of all on his part. "We'll have that again," he said to the chorus, "it won't do you any harm, it will do you good." Zeal, intensity, utter absorption—these are the main ingredients of his methods. When the moment comes to relax, he relaxes as readily, and as completely, as any of his players and singers. Back on the platform, inertia, indifference, slackness are cast out like devils, but usually there is no need for exorcism. The devils know better than to gate-crash.

It is a warm, sunny personality with which he confronts the world and his work. The vitality he expends would furnish half a dozen "going concerns." See him among his friends, off duty, and he warms them up as he does an orchestra. Some people suck vitality from you. Barbirolli charges your own batteries for you, enjoys the process, and sends you home feeling you are not a bad sort of fellow really. But, if you are in his orchestra, don't fluff that phrase next morning, for if you do you may be made to feel that perhaps . . . well, you know! His dynamic concentration is inexhaustible. It has a tingling quality, and it comes over to the audience even in the vastnesses of Belle Vue. His platform manner is smooth and graceful. The baton lines are clear and the symmetry of his style a pleasure to the eye. His left hand always reminds you that he was a 'cellist before he was a conductor, and his whole professional demeanour that he is a natural and devoted musician.

You cannot be a "personality" without evoking criticism. John Barbirolli is no exception. But you must accept his sincerity even if you want to argue about his interpretation. He will listen as readily as he has always learned, but you will be wise to have your facts substantiated and your argument clear. His convictions go deep, and he is not to be moved by changing fashions and whims of taste.

He looks as young and fresh to-day as he did years ago, and this youthful appearance and his shock of black hair make it difficult to remember how wide an experience, in operatic and symphonic conducting, he has had. One always goes to his concerts with a feeling of sharp expectancy. They are so alive.

SIR THOMAS BEECHAM, whose return from America adds another gratifying excitement to concert-going, is individualist *par excellence*. I have heard orchestral players say that he "mesmerises" them into excellence. He has something of that effect on the audience too. Who among lovers of music has not waited for his stately walk to the stand, noting the cool, almost arrogant imperturbability of it, and then the elegant, deliberately leisured bow, first to the audience, then to the orchestra? "Tommy," we say to ourselves, "is back . . ." Before long, the orchestra boils and the magic spells are weaving. Sir Thomas cannot be discussed in terms of conventional technique. He makes his own. It reminds me of the fencer, that sudden lunge of the baton, which has almost a physical effect even though you are behind it, in the auditorium. Then that flashing flick of his wrist is to conducting what the flick of his tongue is to public speech.

In a work to which he is devoted the fire of his temperament has a fascinating effect, but the controlling brain is ice-cool. Note how from the Olympian detachment of the moment before the music begins he catapults himself into the centre of the battle. On one or two occasions I have sat in the orchestra seats, facing Beecham. His face, when he is in action, is hypnotically expressive and compelling. All of him seems to be living the music: the tense crouch, the hissing for a *pianissimo*, the urgent sweep of the right arm, the miming in a dainty, dance-like movement, and finally the two-fisted assault on the orchestra at the climax. Here is heterodoxy at white heat.

There is nothing new that can be said about this extraordinary man, for we have long known and enjoyed his art, but each fresh appearance he makes still has the quality of a shattering début. His memory, of course, is fantastic, like Toscanini's or Sabata's, and it is seldom that he uses a score. Orchestral players unfamiliar with his methods no doubt often find him difficult to follow. Bernard Shore, in *The Orchestra Speaks*, says that "he breaks every orthodox rule. No one else in the world could get away with it as he does." Safety first has never been his motto.

His rehearsals are usually quiet, and invariably productive of a few good laughs. His wit always sparkles, and the stories that cluster about his name and fame are legion. Most conductors cannot be imagined in any other rôle. Beecham, with his brilliance, his audacity, his wit, his oratorical gifts, would have been an outstanding figure and "character" in several other spheres of human activity.

I can imagine Barbirolli, Beecham, or Sabata getting tired after a strenuous season and looking forward to a holiday. But though a pianist, unlike a conductor, sits still (more or less) on the platform, I cannot imagine ARTUR SCHNABEL ever getting tired, strenuous as is the life of a world-famous pianist. Schnabel has altered very little since I last saw him, some years ago. His hair has grown whiter, but he conveys the same impression of thick-set power. He bows as stiffly, sits at the piano as one who confers a favour upon it (and us), and plays. He does not appear to expend any effort even in the most exacting programme, unless you call his familiar little grunts—whether of self-criticism or self-approval, I don't know—a kind of effort.

Critics vary much in their judgment of his performances, and by critics I do not mean only those who are professional writers on music. To some he has always been a pianistic monarch who can do no wrong. Others have said he is "too intellectual," or too indifferent to architectural outline, and so on. So be it. He himself does not worry what they think. He plays the piano, smokes his cigars, and goes his way, masterfully, at 64, with a tough indifference to the disputations he may arouse.

His fellow-practitioners seldom miss an opportunity to hear him. I have heard him described as a "pianist's pianist" and as a "musician's musician." Other pianists and musicians pay him the compliment of going to his concerts—a not insignificant phenomenon. His aloofness may well add to his power to compel interest. Even in private you are conscious of that aloofness. His devotion to the great masters is as inflexible as his unconcern about publicity. He has no public poses or tricks. He does not attempt to propitiate or amuse. "Here is a Beethoven Sonata, and this is how I play it. You do not like it that way? Ah, well..."

Whether you like it or not, you cannot ignore this uncompromising artist who when practising a sonata with Einstein (of Relativity fame) reproached the famous mathematician with his inability to count properly! That is typical of the man. He is never overawed. The tablets of his dogma cannot be readily chipped. It is clear that such a man will not evoke constant adulation. He is provocative. I know, for I have spent many hours in recent years listening to, and participating in, arguments for and against Schnabel as an interpreter. It would be dull and sterilising if all artists created a kind of smug satisfaction. Let us, now and then, be shaken into discontent—even if it be not divine.

Burly, smiling geniality is the first impression one has of GREGOR FITELBERG, the Polish conductor. I met him a few hours after he arrived in London from America, just before the International Festival of Contemporary Music, and he was so obviously delighted to be in England that it was almost embarrassing to listen to his tribute to our courage and endurance in the war and to our poise and friendliness in the peace. I tried to tell him that we were tired and shabby and edgy—rather below ourselves generally—but he waved all that aside and just beamed with pleasure. He was in London; what more could anyone want?

Strongly built, thick-set, his grey hair enhances the dignified, tranquil intellectuality of his appearance. Unobtrusive on the rostrum, he has an authoritative competence that reminds me of the unshowy efficiency of Henry Wood. Off duty, he is charming, animated, and obviously fond of life. You feel better for knowing him.

BRAINS TRUST

Julian Herbage

*

Q. "How far should a great conductor impose his personality in his reading of a great musical work, say Beethoven's Ninth Symphony?"

A. A grand question. I have taken it first because it is both fundamental and controversial. Let us get it on the broadest possible basis, and realise at the start that music does not exist until it is *performed*, whatever our armchair score-readers may say to the contrary. Indeed, an Indian musician would tell you to-day that written-out music is merely an exercise for students, and that real music is entirely extemporised—a spontaneous act of creation by the performer himself. Nevertheless, we in the West have gradually acclimatised ourselves to an individual called the composer who has concentrated on writing down with gradually increasing accuracy the musical ideas which the performer (no longer necessarily a composer himself) has to "interpret." Three centuries ago a composer was normally his own performer, and was reluctant to publish his compositions, because he was afraid that rivals would steal his musical ideas. Even when he did venture into print, he would publish merely the skeleton of his composition, and would never dream of including those embellishments which he would extemporise at performance. Only within the last hundred years, and only in the Western hemisphere, has music become a written-out art of which the printed notes are sacred and inviolable. Wagner parodied this tendency when he created the character of Beckmesser, the armchair critic *par excellence*, who knew all about rules, but nothing about inspiration.

Our present questioner, however, is presumably inquiring about music as it exists in the Western world to-day. Since the era of Nikisch and Richter we have been living in the age of the virtuoso conductor. His job is not to make music himself, but to make others make it. What should be his qualifications? Ernest Newman has compactly summarised them as "composer-psychology, style-analysis, and period-æsthetics." Those are the laboratory methods which he should use to study his scores—his performance should be the result of the feeling and conviction derived from that study. If he does not interpret a work with every atom of understanding and expression of which he is capable, I consider he has failed as an artist. I would never have him restrain himself out of "reverence" to a composer's supposed wishes. If he does not feel, and is not convinced, he had better leave the music alone. I need hardly add that any attempt to focus attention upon himself rather than on the music is pure charlatanism.

Q. "Why is modern music so difficult to understand?"

A. One is reminded of the indignant clubman who complained that *Punch* was no longer as good as it used to be, to be countered with the reply "But it never was!" That, however, is merely the answer which I would give to those who say that modern music is not worth understanding. For those who wish to understand it, and are still baffled, one must go deeper into the matter. Firstly, we must realise that the human mind reacts against the acceptance of new ideas. Philosophers and scientists throughout the ages have been persecuted for them. Taking the case of music, when Monteverdi published his *System of Discords* over three hundred years ago, the whole host of critics took up arms against him. Yet in time his theories became current practice, and were included in even the most academic text-books of composition. Similar storms were aroused by the music of nearly every great composer, particularly Beethoven, Wagner, and Debussy. To-day a slavish imitation of the styles and idio-syncrasies of these masters is the sign of the student or the academic composer. These styles and developments have been uncon-sciously absorbed into our musical vocabulary until by themselves they are now meaningless conventionalities. As composers strive to penetrate unexplored fields of musical expression, they invariably encounter this conservative reaction against the unfamiliar. History may indeed repeat itself, but only in the perpetual war of old against new ideas. Of course, ideas are not good simply because they are new, and there are as many bad composers and charlatans to-day as there ever were in music—possibly more, since a high standard of technique is a rarity nowadays. And so our present confused age, with composers pulling in different ideological and technical directions, will eventually sort itself out by the process of time, and future generations will be able to detect in it the course of what Professor Tovey happily described as "the main stream of music.' Meanwhile, my advice to those who find modern music difficult to understand is to study old music, or Oriental music, or indeed any music of which the idiom is unfamiliar. In this way you will get a flexible mind and understanding, and will no longer feel baffled by any music which does not conform to your own idea of the conventional and familiar.

Q. "What do you consider the most interesting instrument of the orchestra—and why?"

A. Of course I must say the violin. In the first place, it is the leader of the string family, and the string family is the basis of the orchestra. It is the instrument with the largest range; it can be bowed, plucked, muted, or produce harmonics, and about the only thing you cannot do is to blow it, and no doubt some modern composer will include even that instruction in his score soon! Rossini has even used the bow tapped on the desk as a musical effect in his *Signor Bruschino* Overture, and the varieties of tone-colour when the bow is used on the strings are innumerable—one need only mention the macabre effect of bowing near the bridge known as "sul ponticello." One of the violin's most fascinating features is that the two hands are used for different purposes, the right to produce the note, and the left to alter the pitch, and provide a vibrato which can be adjusted at will from a cold, steady tone to a throb of emotional intensity which is perhaps even more effective in quiet than in loud passages. One of the secrets of Toscanini is that he insists on *pianissimos* always being "warm"—that is, played with vibrato. The violin can play up to four notes at once, its agility is unparalleled, its singing quality unsurpassed. Most great conductors, if not violinists, have at least been string players, because a knowledge of the possibilities of string technique is the fundamental issue in orchestral playing. Even an eminent military band conductor once told me to phrase the parts for wind instruments exactly as I would phrase similar passages for the strings.

Q. "Why is Beethoven considered to have had such a great effect on contemporary composers?"

A. Frankly I do not understand the question. If the questioner means *Beethoven's* contemporaries, as far as I know Beethoven's music merely succeeded in making most of them feel hot under the collar. Even his admirers could only refer to "uncommon passages" or "abstruse scientific modulations." If, however, the word "contemporaries" refers to composers alive to-day, I would say it is upon present-day audiences rather than composers that Beethoven produces such a great effect. There is no doubt that during the war Beethoven's spiritual philosophy found a unique response among those who crowded our concert-halls. Beethoven, like Churchill, provided a creed of courage, an unquenchable belief in the power of individual man to mould his destiny and achieve the highest paths of brotherhood. If any composer to-day wished to speak a similar message, he would hardly dare to follow Beethoven's technique, for Beethoven, in his own way, has said the last word. On the contrary, those composers in search of a new technique of expression would certainly go to other masters for guidance. Perhaps Bach is to-day the most influential composer's composer. Schönberg has absorbed him, Stravinsky has flirted with him, and Hindemith has flattered him with sincere imitation. This intellectual Bach cult, begun by Liszt (I am not forgetting Mendelssohn) and continued by

Busoni—considered by some as the father of modern music—has now spent much of its force, and our younger composers are tending to look to Mozart for spiritual guidance. Is it too much to prophesy that the new age of music will aim at the perfection of simplicity? The megalomania of Strauss's age gave way to the complexities of the Central Europeans, but a new era seems to be dawning. One can discern its prophets in many countries.

NEW BOOKS

Reviewed by Stanley Bayliss

*

(1) *British Music of Our Time*. Edited by A. L. Bacharach. Pelican Books. 1s. net.

(2) *Free Thought and the Musician and Other Essays*. Ernest Walker. Oxford University Press. 8s. 6d. net.

(3) *Mussorgsky*. M. D. Calvocoressi. "The Master Musicians" Series. J. M. Dent & Sons Ltd. 6s. 6d. net.

(4) *Opening Bars: Beginning an Autobiography*. By Spike Hughes. Pilot Press Ltd. 10s. 6d. net.

British Music of Our Time is, as its editor, A. L. Bacharach, says, "unabashed propaganda." It is addressed mainly to the home market, for, in spite of the progress made in musical composition in England, the average English music-lover still passes by on the other side. Elgar alone receives any considerable number of performances in our regular concert programmes.

However, as I first saw the book while I was a member of an army of occupation, I was able to try it out on a German musician, and therefore know, at any rate, that Ralph Hill's article on Delius created some interest. But what, I wonder, would a foreigner make of the verbosity of Robin Hull on Eugène Goossens?

The English reader will probably think that the panegyric is occasionally pitched a little too high. Does that matter? A Dutch officer, not unsympathetic to English music, once told me that if the Continent thinks the English are an inartistic nation, it is our own fault. We don't blow our own trumpets loud enough.

Of the eighteen pieces of advocacy contained in this book, by far the most satisfactory is that on Gustav Holst by Gerald Abraham. His was a difficult task in that he wanted to place a high valuation upon a composer whose fame at the moment is markedly lower than it was at the close of his life. Surveying calmly and not uncritically Holst's life and works and such paramount influences as his study of Sanskrit literature, Mr. Abraham succeeds, I think, in persuading us that "the mature Holst" was "one of the most truly 'original' and individual composers of the twentieth century."

In some of the other essays there is a fair amount of loose writing. In "Mixed Gallery," for instance, Edward Lockspeiser discusses, amongst others, Joseph Holbrooke. Now, Mr. Lockspeiser is perfectly entitled to his opinion as to the value of Holbrooke's music, but, in writing it down, doesn't he indulge in some illegitimate judgments? Holbrooke's "string quartets," he says, "are given odd titles—*Pickwick Club*, for instance, and *Byron*." Why is this odd? Fundamentally, it is no more absurd for Holbrooke to write a string quartet having as programme Dickens's *Pickwick Papers* than it is for Strauss to write a tone poem on Cervantes' *Don Quixote*, or Elgar a symphonic study of Shakespeare's Falstaff. If Mr. Lockspeiser wants to say Holbrooke's quartet is of no great musical worth, why doesn't he say so, instead of making an illegitimate criticism of its title? Again, in the same chapter, he has to discuss Balfour Gardiner's "Shepherd Fennel's Dance," which is based on an episode in one of Hardy's "Wessex Tales." "Through the music of Vaughan Williams," he remarks, "we have since acquired a different musical conception of Hardy." Is he thinking of Holst's *Egdon Heath*? As far as I can remember, none of Vaughan Williams's music is associated with Hardy, though he wrote a Pastoral Symphony, The Lark Ascending (Meredith), and set the verses of a Dorset poet, William Barnes, to music.

The earliest essay in Ernest Walker's *Free Thought and the Musician and Other Essays* is dated 1901, the latest 1933. It is astonishing how apposite many of these articles still are. Next year, for instance, will see the centenary of the death of Mendelssohn, and it is very improbable that anyone will contest the judgment Dr. Walker passed upon him when he wrote of the centenary of Mendelssohn's birth. "Mendelssohn's finest music," he writes, "always seems to be the work of a great genius of the age of somewhere between seventeen and twenty—even the 'Hebrides' Overture is still the work of a youth, in a graver mood. Much of it, indeed, actually dates from those years; but even if a little later, there are still the moods of one who has put away childish things but is not yet a full-grown man—the buoyant freshness and frankness, the healthy delight in nature, the first stirring of sincere emotion which has as yet had no time to be deep." With the Dr. Walker of 1909 we still have to remark upon how seldom we are allowed to hear Mendelssohn's other "water pictures"—the *Calm Sea and Prosperous Voyage* and *Melusina* Overtures. How many concert-goers, he asks, would recognise the quotation from the former in Elgar's *Enigma* Variations if the programme analyst did not point out the fact to them?

Then, when we are exasperated by ballets that are composed to abstract music such as Brahms's Fourth Symphony, we may turn to *The Tyranny of the Dance*, written in 1914 after the amalgamation of the Oxford Folk-music Society with the Oxford branch of the English Folk-dance Society. It is refreshing to hear the old English Puritan speaking out: "Art demands life; but all life surely tends towards self-control, towards the ruling of nerve and muscle by mind, towards something of the Stoic and the Puritan; and the higher music is, the less it is visibly (or verbally) expressible. To submit a spiritual art to a bodily tyranny is to deny the past that has made us."

The latest addition to Dent's invaluable "Master Musicians" series is M. D. Calvocoressi's *Mussorgsky*. It is ironical that it was left unfinished through the lamented death of its author, since all but one of the operas of its subject were also left unfinished. The task of completing the book for publication devolved upon Gerald Abraham, Calvocoressi's co-worker in the study of Russian music. Fortunately we need not liken his labours to those of Rimsky-Korsakov upon *Boris Godunov*. All his contributions are enclosed between square brackets. He also tells us that there is a big definitive work by Calvocoressi on Mussorgsky lying in a Paris safe, awaiting the day when conditions will make its publication possible. Meanwhile, this little book furnishes an admirable survey of Mussorgsky's life and work.

Spike Hughes has had a lively life, and his autobiography, *Opening Bars*, makes lively reading. It is also often tiresome. We hear too many times the same jocular remarks about homosexuals; and he also tells us too many times that he is lazy and therefore appreciates application and hard work in others. In spite of all his flippancy and (dare I say it?) thoughtlessness, there is a good deal of sound musical sense in his book, especially on the interpretation of Mozart.

Like his father, Herbert Hughes, he has been a musical critic, and it is amusing to note that he has experiences similar to oneself and in one case has held the same office! Nevertheless, he is a little unjust to his former colleagues. In comparing the lot of the dramatic critic with that of the music critic, he points out that the former deals almost entirely with the performance of new pieces, whereas the latter is principally confined to writing about performances of old and established works. Is that the music critic's fault? I am certain that most of us are only too pleased to write about new works. Then, in discussing the English attitude to music-making, Mr. Hughes accuses the critics of indulging the cult of the amateur. He writes: " 'Sincerity' is a term of justification to which English critics are touchingly devoted. They would rather hear my German pianist, Herr Icks, floundering about his Steinway, dropping wrong notes as the R.A.F. dropped incendiaries, because his Beethoven is 'sincere' (and inaccurate), than hear Heifetz playing a Wieniawski concerto. But then most English critics are determined never to enjoy music; to play something correctly and in tune is rather bad form; it shows that somebody has bothered to acquire a technique. In England, of course, music comes primarily from the Soul; only the blundering amateur is 'sincere' and above suspicion."

That is nonsense. Heifetz playing Wieniawski and Menuhin playing Paganini give all critics a great deal of pleasure; but surely critics may be pardoned for preferring to find the former sponsoring the Walton Concerto and the latter Bártok's Concerto? My own experience of the Continent is very small in comparison with Mr. Hughes's—in fact, it is almost confined to the last two years!—but, to my mind, quite a number of German critics are prepared to write polite notices of downright bad playing and bad German players are just as touchy as our own people about outspoken criticism!

NEW MUSIC

Robin Hull

*

I am delighted to find that most publishers are giving a leading
place to notable works by British composers of our time. Some
of these works were first heard during the war, but few of us
were free to attend the performances, and those who did rarely
had any means of checking their impressions. The scores I am
reviewing here help to meet this need, and provide a revealing
glimpse of recent developments in British music. This is not to
overlook the fact that other countries have made important contributions during and since the war. I hope to deal chiefly with
American and Continental works in the next issue.

The long-awaited score of Vaughan Williams's Fifth Symphony (O.U.P., 12s. 6d.) is a model of clear printing and first-
rate production. I emphasise these points with good reason.
Publishers seem often to forget that miniature or reduced scores
must be *legible*; their whole purpose is nullified if the music-
lover has to examine them through three pairs of spectacles.
The four movements of the Symphony—Preludio, Scherzo,
Romanza, Passacaglia—are superbly integrated, and in general
the work strikes me as an almost perfect summing-up of Vaughan
Williams's art. The moods are mainly lyrical and deeply medita-
tive; the invention is of exquisite beauty; and the expression of
this beauty ranges from downright virility to an enchanting
tenderness. The music has some affinity to his Pastoral Symphony,
but is much more than a reversion to that vein. These contem-
plative pages suggest, rather, a solution to the stark problems
that remained at the close of No. 4 in F minor. It is not too
fanciful, perhaps, to feel that the Fifth Symphony enshrines the
vision of a world liberated from evil. Not everyone will agree
with this view of its mystical quality. And I don't suggest that

the Symphony is flawless. The muffled scurry of the Scherzo never quite makes its point, even in an excellent performance, and I think this arises from the orchestral treatment. Again, the final passage of the Passacaglia can strike one as over-smooth and too easy-going truly to clinch so momentous an argument. It is not the place for a grand gesture, certainly, but the question remains whether Vaughan Williams's ending returns the full answer that the Symphony as a whole leads us to expect.

Though some of Gordon Jacobs's shorter works are familiar to a very wide public, his music on a larger scale is less well known than it deserves. It is puzzling, for instance, that we have not had more performances of his exceedingly fine *Variations on an Original Theme* (Joseph Williams, 10s.). The theme itself is attractive and finely shaped, and the composer turns it to splendid account in his nine well-contrasted variations. These are wrought with true imagination, the musical interest being kept at a high level, and each is set out to expert advantage. It goes almost without saying that the orchestration is consistently skilful. More important is the genuine and vivid originality of Jacobs's invention. The third variation, for instance, reveals an apt combination of strength and breadth that may surprise those chiefly acquainted with his lighter works. Where speed and brilliance are called for (as in the sixth variation), these qualities are forthcoming in an impressive degree. The most remarkable feature of all, to my mind, is Jacobs's really magnificent fugue at the close—no academic jugglery, this, but the natural and imposing culmination to a memorable score.

Three different facets of British music to-day are shown in a group of potent compositions for solo instrument and orchestra. Among these, E. J. Moeran's Rhapsody in F sharp for piano and orchestra (J. & W. Chester, 7s.) offers a welcome alternative indeed to some of the older concertos which have been worn threadbare up and down the country. Here is a Rhapsody that really lives up to its title. Moeran is one of the few living composers who can handle this kind of pattern with true mastery.

He writes succinctly and often brilliantly, giving due place to lyrical meditation, and achieves a feeling of spaciousness without the slightest deviation into relaxed or diffuse thought. He scores for a fairly large orchestra, but these resources are used economically, and leave him an ample reserve for moments of heightened power. His treatment of the keyboard, too, is both expert and closely sympathetic; to be sure, the music calls for first-rate playing, alike in matters of technique and interpretation, yet its demands on the player are wholly reasonable. My own view is that Moeran finds himself thoroughly at home in a work conceived on this scale (the duration of the Rhapsody is 17½ minutes). He has given us some glorious music, of course, in the two concertos proper—for violin and violoncello respectively—but here the pattern seems even more to his liking. Moreover, the Rhapsody is an ideal length for many programmes in which, frankly, the listener does *not* want a three-movement concerto in addition to a big symphony. Whether anything will induce builders of programmes to realise this fact, and turn aside from the beaten track, is a problem which seems to fall within the province of brain specialists!

It is curious and interesting that Walton's Violin Concerto (O.U.P., 12s. 6d.) has been much slower to establish itself than one might expect from the success of his other big-scale works—*Belshazzar's Feast* and the Symphony, for instance—or even from the aggregate merits of the Violin Concerto itself. My impression is that this composition was partially and quite needlessly handicapped from the start by the fantastic blaze of publicity which heralded its first performance in England. The result of such an ill-judged "build-up" was that the public expected nothing less than a resounding masterpiece, eclipsing even the genius of the Symphony, and there was a considerable sense of disappointment that the Concerto fell short of these absurd anticipations. Judged from the angle of to-day, the Violin Concerto stands out as a work of very high quality, though I cannot share the view that it is the best work Walton has written.

The strength of the invention lies much in its unfaltering unity. The musical pattern unfolds with an inevitable logic, and the result is that the three movements form a truly organic pattern. Again, the ideas from which this design takes shape are bold and arresting. Their treatment keeps a firm grip on the listener's attention, and the writing for solo instrument, though making exceptional demands upon virtuosity, is always integral to the composer's purpose. In the face of these virtues, one may well ask why the Concerto has not made more substantial headway. One reason may be that, compared with the Symphony, there seems to be an insufficient urgency of address. This, in turn, appears to arise from the fact that Walton contents himself with familiar ground rather than the fresh adventures to be expected after the Symphony. For my part, I cannot escape the view that the Symphony left some vital problems to be solved before Walton could genuinely advance on his path as composer, and that the Concerto postpones a reckoning with these problems.

I have said elsewhere that the gifts of Alan Rawsthorne may yet stand in evident range of equality with those of Benjamin Britten. There are signs that that opinion is being steadily justified by events, but its formation required no special perspicuity. Readers may like to examine some of the evidence for themselves now that we have the score of Rawsthorne's Concerto for piano and orchestra (O.U.P., 7s. 6d.). A certain amount of dissent was expressed by people who found this work "difficult" at first hearing, but it has also succeeded in arousing and holding the interest of many who do not consider themselves high-flying specialists. The fascination of the music lies, first and foremost, in the fact that it comes from an intensely original, vivid, and thoughtful mind. The so-called "difficulty" is of the kind that yields quite swiftly to applied listening; all three movements are thoroughly stimulating and the final "Tarantella" is genuinely light-hearted. But I have every sympathy with listeners who complain that a paucity of performances does make close familiarity with the Concerto hard to achieve. Here, surely, is a cast-iron case for demanding that the work should be recorded for gramophone. This is a paramount instance in which the British Council might attempt to exert themselves, and even proceed to the extremity of helpful action. Being an eternal optimist, I hope that somebody has already realised the urgency of the situation, and that a recording may be imminent by the time this article is published.

The firm of Lengnicks have shown great enterprise in publishing a stout batch of works by Charles Proctor. These include a Sonata in D minor for organ, a Sonata in A minor for violin and piano, and a number of songs—the prices, I think, are not given, or at any rate they have escaped my vigilance. I examined these works with great interest, but with a feeling of declining confidence about their significance. Their pages include very many of the qualities essential for good composition. The Violin Sonata, for example, makes clear that the composer has a real gift for lyrical melody—an immense virtue, that—and his craftsmanship is above reproach in every work I have studied. The factor which strikes rather hard at the importance of this and the other sonatas is twofold: a really fine opening is apt to subside into figuration of too formal a kind, and the promising flow of invention does tend to shape itself as exceedingly well-written extemporisation. But the music itself is always agreeable, and in the songs—particularly the set entitled "Four Various Songs"—the inspiration is more evenly sustained. I can imagine that all these works would give much pleasure as home-music, especially among capable players, and I am sure they can fulfil a real need of that kind. It would be less fair to pit these compositions against the sterner standards relevant to the music discussed in my earlier paragraphs. There is ample room in the world for all of them.

THE RECORD COLLECTOR

Alec Robertson

★

I HAVE long been of the opinion that the regular purchaser of gramophone records, whatever kind of music he may be interested in, is, in general, the most intelligent and best-informed of all music-lovers, and certainly the keenest.

There are many reasons for this. In the concert-hall there is always something to disturb concentrated listening. Is the singer really feeling the strain as much as his agonised expression makes it appear, and will he presently be carried out in a fit? Is the pianist's memory about to fail her, or does her countenance merely betray an intense dislike of the instrument upon which she is inflicting such punishment? Will the violinist, at present mopping his brow, get his instrument back into position in time for the entry which is drawing so perilously near? And so on. And the audience, how can one fail to be distracted by the audience! How comes it that the apparently newly engaged couple just in front of me have chosen a performance of Beethoven's *Hammerklavier* Sonata (clearly advertised outside the hall) as a background for their mutual endearments and confidences, and why should they choose to display them in this excessively well-lit and expensive interior rather than in the decent and free obscurity of the adjacent park? Must that blue-haired dowager drop her umbrella during the quietest part of the slow movement, and leave the hall at a precisely similar moment later on: must people rustle newspapers, cough, whisper, and even be sick? From all these and other disturbances which my eyes have perforce witnessed during the last few weeks may the good Lord deliver us, as He has delivered the occupant of the armchair by the fireside who, perhaps at such very moments, alone or in chosen company, has been listening to his music undisturbed. I say rightly to *his* music, for, though at second-hand, it is indeed his; he has acquired his records, it may well be, at the price of considerable hardship and self-sacrifice.

It is no wonder, therefore, that the record collector, who has built up his library at the cost of going without many ordinary pleasures, should be concerned to get the utmost out of it, and in so doing—because he really gets to know the music to which he listens—qualify for the title of the best-informed and most intelligent of music-lovers.

I doubt if we fully appreciate yet the tremendous influence of the gramophone in spreading the musical gospel, in creating a genuine artistic democracy and a most delightful freemasonry. It is indeed striking to see this revolutionary change in the musical scene when one remembers how, only twenty-five years ago, the gramophone was almost universally despised by professional musicians and had a repertoire, especially in the instrumental field, of the most meagre kind.

To-day, though there are exasperating gaps in the catalogues, and even more exasperating yearly deletions, most of the basic classical works have been recorded, and we receive a fair and increasing proportion of contemporary music. But the position is far from satisfactory. The gramophile, to-day, is not merely content to listen to his records, he builds up, also, a library of books on music, and of scores; and as his knowledge grows he finds the apparent lack of planning and co-ordination among the gramophone companies peculiarly irritating.

A commercial company which has to consider, amongst other things, its shareholders can always say, in reply to criticism, that it is not a benevolent institution and that deletions are only made because sales are insufficient to keep the records in the catalogues. Matrices are not destroyed; and if a customer has an ungovernable urge for a record, he can purchase a special pressing—at a price; but a price few of us can afford. I must confess, though I know little of the economics of the business, that it is difficult to suggest any solution to the problem, and one can only lament the yearly massacre of the innocents and jealously treasure the deleted records we are fortunate enough to possess.

It would be too much to suggest that every record, as every book, should go to an equivalent of the British Museum; but we have only to think what it would be like to have records of the past at our disposal, to hear, for example, how Bach or Handel played the clavichord or the organ, to realise that it is impossible to set enough store on the recorded performances of outstanding artists to-day.

The economic factor apart, there are many recordings, at present in private hands or issued abroad, one would be thankful to have. Dr. Ludwig Koch's exquisite recordings of two organs upon which Bach played evoked widespread enthusiasm when broadcast, and I should have thought that they, at least, were a commercial proposition. And there are many other things of the same kind. Why, again, have those most lovely records of the Monteverdi Madrigals never been issued over here, or the records of the Couperin *Tenebrae*? There is an atmosphere about these "realisations" by Nadia Boulenger which is usually absent from our choral recordings. Then there are the "Society" recordings. Surely it should be possible, before long, to extract the cream, at least, of these recordings and issue them to the general public in some way or other.

The gramophone companies cannot be unaware that all over the world, wherever our Forces happened to be, a large or small gramophone society came into being and brought, for the most part, an entirely new public into touch with the gramophone. The potentialities are therefore enormous; and though the general needs of this new public can, no doubt, easily be satisfied, I hope that the particular needs of the minority who care for *lieder*, chamber-music, early sacred and secular music, unrepresented contemporary composers, will not be forgotten.

I met at a party, a year or so ago, a tough Canadian soldier who, to my utter surprise, confessed to a passion for those same

Monteverdi records, which he had come across by chance. He had gone on to collect recordings of all the music of the period, few enough, that he could lay hands upon, and was now in the first flush of enthusiasm for the music of the great poly-phonic writers. It is such enthusiasm which keeps this music alive, and it is one of the most valuable functions of the gramophone to nourish it.

Future possibilities, given a little imagination, and the taking of us, by the companies, a little more into their confidence, are indeed exciting. Reproducing instruments are improving as much as recording has improved, and of this there is great need; for the standard of reproduction with which people appear to be content, even very musical people, is far from satisfactory.

The companies, in these last years, have developed something of an artistic conscience, at least in regard to serious music, and the day of cut works, though not of inaccurate labels, is past; but there is still occasion for artists to remind themselves of the semi-permanent character of a recording and not to pass a disc with which they are not satisfied. They should take as their motto the words that Elgar wrote on the score of *The Dream of Gerontius*— "This is the best of me." With such words in mind, I cannot think that Heifetz could have listened to the records he made recently of the Dvořák *Humoreske*, or Iturbi to his recording of the dances from Falla's *El Amor Brujo*, without turning them down flat. A well-known conductor told me the other day that he never listened to the recordings he made because he would at once want to remake them; but though I respect his motive for refusing to hear his discs, it is surely a mistaken one. Since it is impossible to include a review of new records in this number, it may be worth recalling, by way of a postscript, some of the magnificent recordings we have been given since the start of this year up to the month of June.

Singing may be in the doldrums, but in Ada Alsop there seems to be a perfect singer of Handel and a voice that takes naturally to the wax. Axel Schotz has shown himself a fine singer of *lieder* in the *Dichterliebe*, with Gerald Moore as the accompanist; and Poulenc's setting of the two Aragon poems, done by Bernac with the composer at the piano, was another lovely record. The singers have, in fact, far outshone the pianists. In the orchestral field there are the most exciting recordings—in their different way—of Stravinsky's *Petrushka*, with which the London Philharmonic Orchestra made its début, under Ansermet, on Decca, and Berlioz's *Harold in Italy*, William Primrose, Kussevitsky and the Boston Symphony Orchestra on H.M.V.; and of course the new recording of Strauss's *Tyl Eulenspiegel* by the same orchestra and conductor. The newly formed and admirable Philharmonia Orchestra, under Walter Susskind, accompanied Ginette Neveu in her superb performance of the Sibelius Violin Concerto, with which may be linked the equally fine performance of Falla's "Nights in the Gardens of Spain" by Clifford Curzon, Jorda, and the National Symphony Orchestra. But we want more, much more, and much cheaper in price. I hope we do not have to wait long for the Bartók Violin Concerto and the Concerto for Orchestra; or the Interludes and Passacaglia from *Peter Grimes*, though it should be remembered that Britten, who has been well served by Decca, is not the only English composer. The new Pianoforte Trio by Arnold Bax, a lovely work, and Bliss's *Checkmate* suite should not be forgotten. I hope the policy of recording young artists will be continued, but with a repertoire that does not challenge great performances already on the catalogues. There are plenty of other works waiting to be done, and these artists should be encouraged to learn them.

When I write again in these pages, some of these expectations may, I hope, be fulfilled; and some surprises, too, may have been sprung upon us. We shall, we happy band of gramophiles, be well able to support anything of the kind, and I do not think we should drop dead if a long-playing record was announced.

MUSIC ON THE AIR

Richard Gorer

★

INSCRUTABILITY has hitherto been regarded as the prerogative of aged females. Walter Pater, for example, was able to deduce from the inscrutability of the Mona Lisa's smile that she was older than the rocks whereon she sat. Similarly, the smile of the Sphinx is also regarded as inscrutable, though one might be pardoned for supposing that there was nothing very mysterious in a slight trembling of the lips after several centuries of Eygptian tourists. I do not know if there is any aged female responsible for the music policy of the B.B.C., but it is certainly inscrutable. We know that in the commercial world the best things must be reserved for export, but it may come as a surprise to learn that the code of the Board of Trade is valid in Broadcasting House. Thus Honegger's Symphony for strings, which for most listeners received its first performance this year, had in fact been broadcast to France over a year earlier. Again in March in the "Ring up the Curtain" series there were broadcast some excerpts from Smetana's enchanting opera *The Kiss*; previously nearly the whole opera had been performed for the benefit of those listeners to the B.B.C. who inhabit South America. Now artistic novelty may have little attraction for the music directorate, but I cannot fathom the argument that South Americans are more curious in musical matters than we are, or that Frenchmen were prepared to risk death to hear a new work, when we are not even prepared to risk boredom. By all means let us relay admirable things to our foreign audiences, but as this is nominally done on our licence money I cannot see why they should have all the plums while we are all too often fobbed off with what impresarios have decided is the public taste.

Another strange feature, possibly indicated by some List-

95

eners' Research discovery, is the B.B.C.'s assumption that all
devotees of chamber music either rise very early or retire very
late. It is true that of late it has been possible to hear chamber
music once a fortnight at a reasonable time, but this is an inno-
vation. Since chamber music broadcasts far better than orchestral,
the emphasis that is laid on this latter can scarcely be purely
artistic. It is due, I am informed, to the B.B.C.'s educational
mission. The argument runs as follows: the virgin listener has by
some accident, either by going to the cinema or by not switching
off the wireless rapidly enough, become exposed to some
classical music. To his amazement he is not bored stiff and
eagerly searches the programme so that he may hear this
particular piece again or something else by the same composer
(e.g. *Tapiola* after the *Valse Triste*). Finally, utterly lost to shame,
he takes to music like an addict to a drug. I believe myself this
argument to be fallacious. It is true that most of us progress from
second-rate music to first-rate, but I do not see why there should
be this excessive tenderness towards beginners. It is this attitude
of conscious superiority to the well-meaning ignoramus that is
responsible for the poverty of the public concert repertoire.
It would surely be better to assume that people listen to broadcast music because they enjoy it now, not because they may
enjoy it in two years' time.

In spite of my quibbles it must be agreed that there remains a
handsome balance on the credit side of the ledger, to which we
must now turn. I have already said that I think orchestral
music is overemphasised, and so it is in this sphere that most of
interest takes place. The Music of Our Time series is always
interesting, though recently perhaps there has not been any
very great æsthetic pleasure. It would be a help if the concerts
could be repeated. It is remarkable that the most interesting
musical novelties did not occur in these concerts; there was
nothing, for instance, of the calibre of Bártok's Concerto for
Orchestra, though this is one of the regretted composer's slighter
works. Incidentally, Our Time would appear to be an elastic

period, as one of the items was the masterly fragments from *Wozzeck*. Among the new works we have heard have been several from the Soviet Union, of which the most pleasant was Shaporin's cantata *On the Field of Kulikovo*, which, though thoroughly old-fashioned, was melodious and expertly written. For the rest the Russians seem to be spellbound by folk-songs of the slightest artistic interest and employ them for the most curious purposes. Knipper's suite on Iranian folk-song, though noisy and dull, was legitimate, but what on earth prompted Khachaturian to write such a very dull violin concerto on such very dull Armenian folk-songs? At times, in this latter work, I felt a real artistic spirit was trying to break through, only to be crushed under a melody that Czerny would have rejected from his school of velocity.

Late one Sunday evening we learned that Prokofiev himself had fallen for the latest craze and had composed a string quartet on Caucasian songs. Prokofiev can never be dull, but I trust he will never approach much nearer dullness than in this work. By contrast, the music from Poland was a pleasing surprise. Makla-kiewicz's symphonic poem *Grunwald* could have been composed any time since 1890, but would always have been an impressive work, while Szalowski's Overture had a light-heartedness that is far to seek in contemporary music. The only Czech novelties came via the U.S.A. in the form of a symphony and a piano quintet by Martinu. The Symphony was pleasantly unpreten-tious, but the Quintet caused me to revise my rather low opinion of Martinu. I hope we shall hear it again. From Hungary, besides the Bartók Concerto for Orchestra we had Kodaly's Variations for Orchestra. At a first hearing this seemed rather a disappointing work, but it must be heard again. Germany (again via the U.S.A.) has been represented by Hindemith, who, doubtless owing to some fault in my make-up, bores me blue. On the other hand, I appear to be the only one to have enjoyed the Honegger symphony. Our own novelties can stand up to all we have heard from elsewhere. Among the younger composers I was

M.M. 1—4

particularly pleased with Bernard Stevens's Violin Concerto and the Piano Concerto of Humphrey Searle. This latter work had its first performance at the curious time of 3.30 p.m. It is scarcely tea-time music. Britten's Second Quartet interested me as being the only one of his works that seems in any way to deserve the extraordinary laudations wafted to him by certain critics.

Anyone who had the good luck to listen to one of the "Music of the Masters" concerts in the light programme could have heard the first performance of Mozart's Symphony No. 34 with the minuet that Dr. Einstein insists belongs to it. The enterprising conductor was Anthony Collins. It is typical of the inscrutability to which I have referred that an event which could not fail to be of absorbing interest to all musicians should have been unheralded, played at an inconvenient time on the programme where one does not expect much in the way of novelty. Doubtless Dr. Einstein has excellent reasons for his attribution, but on purely stylistic grounds I felt somewhat doubtful. It is a magnificent composition. The more orthodox concerts are somewhat timid in their repertory and it is rare that you get anything as well balanced as this concert, which was conducted by Sir Adrian Boult: Berlioz, *Overture King Lear*; Dukas, *La Péri*; Sibelius, Symphony No. 7. Both as regards interest and length this might serve as a model. Constant Lambert must be thanked for introducing Balakirev's overture to *King Lear*, and I hope that we shall soon have the entr'actes. I much regret having missed the *Serenade Fantastique* for viola and orchestra by Sainton, for many years leader of the Philharmonic and one of those responsible for Wagner's engagement. Unadventurousness is a term which cannot be applied to the gramophone concerts, which, though nearly always at times when I cannot listen, have the most delectable programmes.

Like all institutions, the B.B.C. is capable of improvements, and I will conclude this review with some suggestions for the betterment of the music department. These fall under four headings:

I. OPERA. The broadcasting of opera is one of the weakest parts of the B.B.C.'s musical service, and too often when an opera is broadcast it is one that is already an established favourite. When only some half-dozen operas are broadcast each year, it seems a pity to perform *La Tosca*, admirable though it is. With the approach of programme C, I cannot see why the B.B.C. should not have a repertory opera company in the same way as they have already a theatrical company. One opera a fortnight would not be excessive, and then there might be a chance for some of our contemporary composers to hear their operas. One performance of Gray's superb *Women of Troy* is not really adequate, and there is the same composer's *Temptation of Anthony*, Van Dieren's *The Tailor*, Vaughan Williams's *Riders to the Sea*, and Benjamin's *Prima Donna* all waiting to be performed. A little more preparation for the listener would not come amiss. The interval talks in the symphony concerts are usually admirable, but there is nothing like them for opera, which must be more unfamiliar than symphony to the majority of listeners.

II. CHORAL MUSIC. For some reason this once traditional English love is now absurdly neglected, with the result that such masterpieces as Berlioz's *Tristia, Romeo and Juliet,* and the fantasy on the *Tempest* are unknown over here. Indeed, there is a vast mine of choral works such as Schumann's *Faust* and *Paradise and the Peri*, Dvořák's *Requiem Mass*, and Janáček's cantatas waiting to be explored.

III. CHAMBER MUSIC. As I have already pointed out, this is under-represented at the present time, although most suitable for broadcasting. The repertoire, too, is restricted to recent works and the classical masterpieces. It would surely be interesting to explore some of the byways such as Cherubini's quartets, Spohr's double quartets, and Marschner's piano trios, to say nothing of the less familiar quartets of Haydn and Mozart.

IV. BRITISH MUSIC. I imagine there is no country that has less knowledge of its own traditions in music than our own. For most of us the period between Purcell and the Parry-Stanford

"Renaissance" is a musical Sahara, and even the masterpieces of earlier days—the works of Byrd, Gibbons, and Dowland—are taken on trust and never performed. If the B.B.C. really feels it has an educational mission, it can fulfil it in this field. I suggest they begin with some of these works: Blow's *Venus and Adonis* (broadcast in the '30s), Lampe's *Dragon of Wantley*, Arne's *Comus*, *Achilles in Petticoats*, *The Fairy Prince*, the cantatas and concerti; Boyce's *Solomon*, Greene's Pastorals, Jackson's Elegies and Pastorals, Chilcot's concerti, that curious precursor of Wagnerism the anonymous music to Mason's *Caractacus*, Storace's *The Pirates*, Hook's *Lady of the Manor*, Shield's Trios, Griffin's quartets, Potter's symphonies, the concerti of Field and of Bennett, and the works of that curious Berlioz-like figure Henry Hugo Pierson. Any one of these works is of as much interest as, for example, the music of Respighi, and it seems disgraceful that for the most part they are unfamiliar and that the scores are not easily accessible. The list could easily be prolonged, but enough has been said to show what a heritage we are missing.

OPERA IN LONDON

Stephen Williams

★

I THINK it was Rossini who laid it down that three qualities were
required to make an opera singer: "voce, voce, e poi voce." We
must remember, of course, that that was in the golden age of
voice-worship, when singers devoted music to themselves instead of devoting themselves to music, and when it was a truism
that the larger the voice the smaller the intellect. To-day the
pendulum has swung to the other extreme. Modern music and
modern production do not demand great voices, and nature,
obedient to art in this as in so many matters, no longer produces
them. Occasional exceptions only prove the rule. The giants
are no more; the great spectacular figures who "trod the boards"
and to whom composers and conductors were on pretty much
the same level as dressers and prompters, have one by one
swaggered and blustered their way into oblivion. Chaliapine
was probably the last of them.

With opera, as with other arts, we are in an age of efficient
mediocrity: efficient, because the general level of intelligent
competence is higher than it was fifty years ago (the old gibe
about "musicians *and* singers" is out of date); mediocrity, because so rarely does one feel the thrill of that unaccountable
thing called genius. And so we make a virtue of necessity: not
having enough "voce" to go round, we reverse Rossini's maxim
and go in for "arte, arte, e poi arte."

There is no more significant example of this than the Sadler's
Wells Company. It was reported, accurately or not, of one of its
producers that he was out "to take the grand out of grand opera."
Again a doctrine of necessity, since there was obviously no one
to put it in. Now the Sadler's Wells Company is at its best in a
work like Britten's *Peter Grimes*, which translates common

speech into uncommon musical forms and which demands not great singing but that alert musicianship and intelligent co-operation in which these artists excel; indeed, Britten has admitted that "the qualities of the Opera Company have considerably influenced both the shape and characterisation of the opera." Similarly, the Company's shortcomings are most evident in a work like Verdi's *Rigoletto*, which demands, not primarily musicianship or co-operation, but sheer singing of the highest virtuosity—in fact, "voce, voce, e poi voce." It is a splendid production and the Company attacks this electric, thunder-and-lightning music with a memorable gusto. (Only those who cannot write a tune themselves sneer at Verdi's brimming melodies.) And yet mere gusto, exhilarating as it is, is not enough: one feels the lack of that ultimate grace, that last refinement of vocal technique that puts a bloom on a phrase, that thins out a sustained note like a thread of gossamer and makes a *diminuendo* as gradual and inevitable as the paling of a star. Compared with the "knotted ganglions" of a score like *Peter Grimes*, early Verdi may seem easy to sing; the answer is that it is fatally easy to sing badly. Still, we certainly had gusto—most memorably from Roderick Jones's Rigoletto and James Johnston as the Duke—a really outstanding tenor whose forthright "Englishness" of style (although he is an Irishman!) made that most odious of operatic bounders almost likeable.

The Company added two fresh works to its repertory in the spring: Vaughan Williams's *Sir John in Love* and *School for Fathers*, a lively and ingenious adaptation by Edward J. Dent of Wolf-Ferrari's *I Quattro Rusteghi*. *Sir John* was ridiculously overpraised, one critic actually likening it to Wagner's *Meistersinger*—a comparison which would probably have embarrassed Vaughan Williams as much as anyone. By all means let us make the most of what operas we have, but panegyrics of that kind defeat their own object and mislead people into expecting more than our English composers can give them. Vaughan Williams cannot give them another *Meistersinger*; but he does give them a very charming picture of mediæval England, fairly faithful to Shakespeare's text (which he supplements with bits of John Still, Ben Jonson, and others), with traditional tunes which are good and original tunes which are excellent. It is a kind of "Falstaff" without Verdi; and one cannot help wondering why Vaughan Williams should so dangerously challenge comparison by setting a subject which Verdi set for all time. Many of the scenes and situations are identical and, fight against it as I would, I found myself listening and longing for the familiar magic. It was the old bottle, but the new wine took a long time to mount to the head. Roderick Jones fluted very mellifluously as the Falstaff— a gentler spirit than the "huge bombard of sack" we meet in *Henry IV*—and Howell Glynne was a solid and formidable Master Ford. Here is a bass of the true quality and power. Another remarkable voice is that of Valetta Iacopi, who sang Dame Quickly: the tone is full and incisive, with a distinct edge to it—perhaps rather too distinct: she is sometimes inclined to "hoot" a little. (That sounds unchivalrous, but no other word could so precisely convey my meaning.)

School for Fathers is an uproarious piece of horseplay with quiet interludes of considerable charm. The story (now transferred from Venice to London) is typical eighteenth-century stuff—heavy fathers, nagging mothers, undutiful daughters, lovers in ludicrous disguises laughing at locks. The score, like *Hamlet*, is "full of quotations," some of them intentional, and one is reminded frequently of Verdi and Puccini. Wolf-Ferrari breaks with tradition by writing his four best male parts for the bass voice, and Sadler's Wells rose nobly to the occasion. Howell Glynne (a really excellent characterisation), Sydney Jack, John Higginson, and David Franklin as the four "Rusteghi" (usually translated as "boors") gave us much splendid singing of genuine bass quality; none of your tentative gargles, but real juicy bottom E's! The women had fewer opportunities, but Nora Gruhn in the last act gave a magnificent fireworks display in a long, tongue-blistering tirade which suggested that Professor Dent had read his W. S. Gilbert!

The first world war produced some splendid poetry and music. I never thought this one would, with its soulless mechanisation and its blasting denial of all that humanity stands for; yet "the unconquerable hope" still persists, and the spirit of man has found some soul of goodness even in a thing so evil as Hitler's Europe. Hence *The Partisans*, a new opera by Inglis Gundry dealing with "underground" warfare in an occupied country, and produced by the Workers' Music Association at the St. Pancras Town Hall last May. This is a strong, virile score, modern in idiom, continuous in movement, unconsciously imitative here and there—its more lyrical moments suggest Vaughan Williams, and its strenuous, booming climaxes have a flavour of Holbrooke. Yet I doubt if it will go down to history as the representative opera of the war. I feel that 1939–45 produced a new war-form and consequently demands a new art-form; an art-form that will scrap the heroic conventions of opera just as Hitler's criminal adventure scrapped the heroic conventions of war. Mr. Gundry is by no means old-fashioned, yet his music might be the music of any war.

There was an amateur atmosphere about the production which was perhaps partly due to the surroundings: however handsome the appointments—and the appointments here are very handsome indeed—there is an inescapable aroma of plain living and high thinking about a town hall, so different from the cosy, sinful glamour of a theatre! Then again, the majority of the singers were not quite equal to Mr. Gundry's exacting score: the voice parts are written on spacious, heroic lines and demand voices of a heroic stature. One was conscious now and then of a running jump at a high note and a wobble of relief when the voice had safely perched on it. The one striking exception was Bruce Dargavel as the Partisan Chief—a rich, wine-dark baritone voice worthy of Wagner. We shall hear more of him.

The latest English venture is the New London Opera Company (the leading soprano is from Russia, the leading tenor from America!) which began a season at the Cambridge Theatre in June with Puccini's *La Bohème*. Here, once more, is an opera that needs not only an abundance of "voce," but also a producer of imagination and humour, a loyal team-spirit and, above all, that indefinable but instantly recognisable quality we call *style*. Well, we had all these. Not that the voices were of world-shaking magnitude; on the contrary, they were mostly small. But the singing always *meant* something. Dino Borgioli's production had a glittering vitality and freshness and Alexandre Benois's scenery and costumes gave a new grace to the stage action. In other words, one *did* perceive a consistent *style* in the thing, the artistic taste of a producer conscious always of the impeccable artistry of Puccini. Yes, I wrote "impeccable artistry," and I mean it. Even the academic mind, however much it may shrink in spinsterly horror from what Puccini did, is beginning to admit that he did it supremely well. Yet Professor Dent can bring himself, in a recent article on Mozart, to write of Puccini's "slobbering erotics." Puccini *was* erotic; it was the very life-blood of his music. But he never slobbered; he was too much of an artist. Least of all did he slobber in *La Bohème*; nowhere is his art more tactful and delicate than here, where even the most emotional passages are touched with a kind of cold, silvery starlight that keeps them eternally fresh.

The new Mimi was Daria Bayan, who was graceful and charming and looked the part—not that I ever think that matters —although on the first night her singing rather lacked confidence. Lester Ferguson, the Rudolph, was a dashing fellow with a modest but expressive tenor. Incidentally, Murger insists throughout the book on Rudolph's "deep bass voice"; but Puccini was too intelligent a man of the theatre to make his lover anything but a tenor! A special word of praise to Stanley Pope, as Marcel—the Athos of the party: he sang with a gracious and easeful sense of style and was lovably in character. And that is important: for a bad Marcel may easily spoil a good *Bohème*.

BALLET IN LONDON

Arnold L. Haskell

★

THE first half of this year has seen so much ballet activity of real interest that it is only possible to glance at some of the more important events.

From the point of view of the large decentralised public the formation of the new company for Sadler's Wells, called by the unfortunate name of the Opera-Ballet, is by far the most important event. It means that the smaller provincial centres that could not have accommodated the larger company will now have the possibility of seeing the ballet on tour and also that Lilian Baylis's great ideal of a people's ballet will be carried through. It provides a stepping-stone from the school to Covent Garden, thereby giving us a system as complete as that of any country where the art is State-supported.

This new company is young, enthusiastic, and, of course, a trifle raw in such delicate works as *Promenade*, but both in style and discipline it is far ahead of the original company at the same stage of development. It has already two creations to its credit. Andrée Howard's *Assembly Ball* to Bizet's Symphony is an elegant and witty commentary on the music, a shade long-drawn-out since no choreography can keep pace with symphonic form, and therefore a trifle lacking in climax. It gives just the right opportunities to this young company to dance, led by the experienced June Brae and a male dancer of great charm and virility, Leo Kersley. Andrée Howard has designed her own setting and costumes and has made them, as they should be, a part of her choreography.

The next creation, *Khadra* to Sibelius's *Belshazzar's Feast*, brings a new-comer to choreography in Celia Franca. She has tackled a difficult problem, the Orient; difficult because for so long it seemed as if Bakst and Fokine had said the last word, difficult because of the dangers of the Oriental bazaar approach, so obvious and so tempting. Together with Honor Frost, who designed costumes and setting, she has avoided all those difficulties, going straight to the Persian miniature for inspiration and making a really successful translation into ballet. Franca has devised some true choreography that is nearly always inspired by the music and that is interesting for its own sake, and her grouping is always beautiful. Time will show whether this is one subject that has tempted her or whether she is to join the limited number of true choreographers. The important feature of the production is the extraordinary partnership between choreographer and designer that makes their work into a whole, something that has been rare in our ballet to date, as the work of our French visitors Les Ballets des Champs-Elysées so clearly underlined. The dancing in *Khadra* reached a high level, Anne Seaton and Sheila O'Reilly in particular attracting attention.

The number one company at Covent Garden has also given us two creations. Robert Helpmann's *Adam Zero* to a first-class dramatic score by Arthur Bliss was something of a disappointment after its first strong impact. Symbolism should be used sparingly, and in any case it cannot make up for a lack of choreography. *Adam Zero* is a brilliant stage production that makes skilled use of every stage device, shattering the illusion that ballet has built up. In parts it is moving, in parts truly dramatic, but if it is to have a long life in the repertoire, it needs serious revision as a ballet and the cutting of the rather tedious political allusions that do not fit into the whole. Also an attack on the Church is not in the best of taste. Robert Helpmann himself, June Brae in a number of rôles, Gillian Lynne, and especially David Paltenghi, as the stage manager around whom the whole action revolves, made themselves noticed among the stage-hand supers and the mass of moving scenery; no mean feat.

Frederick Ashton's ballet to Franck's Symphonic Variations

was a complete contrast. Interpreted by six dancers and with no dramatic content, it set out to parallel the music. There is no more musical choreographer at the present time than Ashton. Bolanchin, also a fine musician, tends to over-subtlety and a striving for originality, while Ashton is always the complete master of his medium, the dancers. The result was an artistically exacting work in which Sophie Fedorovitch, the designer, shared. Her simple abstract background formed the link between music and movement, and she has completely mastered the problem of "abstract" costumes, which usually resemble some form of hygienic underwear.

While the "visible music" ballet must remain an exception and can no more point the way to the future than the dance-drama, this work is assured of a very long life in the repertoire.

The large-scale revival of *The Sleeping Beauty* that opened the record ballet season at Covent Garden produced some admirable dancing. Margot Fonteyn, with an attack that few suspected, was outstanding. Few ballerinas can give so much humanity to a classical rôle. She made the episode of the pricked finger, for instance, into a really moving scene, where it is usually treated as a rest from dancing. Also, she is rare among contemporary dancers for the finish in her movements; she dances right up to her finger-tips.

A comparative novice, Moyra Shearer, caused a balletic sensation by her dancing of the ballerina rôle. She has great beauty, natural grace, and a self-assurance that is unusual in a British dancer. In a year when she has gained technical mastery she should become quite outstanding.

Oliver Messel's setting and costumes are tasteful and always pleasing to the eye, though they lack the theatrical quality— perhaps, in part, vulgarity—that made the Bakst production so outstanding.

In the many revivals, all improved by the size of Covent Garden's stage, Julia Farron's interpretation of the prostitute in *Miracle of the Gorbals* stood out a mile. This young dancer, who early on lost her way as classical ballerina, has emerged as a balletic actress of great quality. Her Estrella in *Carnaval*, most fragile of ballets, was in the true Fokine tradition. In the *Miracle* she uses Helpmann's magnificent material to the full and really creates a character "in the round."

The success of Sadler's Wells has revived the futile controversy about the respective merits of British and Russian dancers. In all these controversies, even when they are genuine and not dictated by some political ideology, there is the use of such vague words as "temperament" and "personality." There can, of course, be no common ground of comparison between a new venture and an old tradition, or between dancers of different generations. With Fonteyn, Helpmann, Grey, Shearer, Clayden, and Farren, to quote but a few names, we have dancers of exceptional quality judged by all contemporary standards. The *prima ballerina assoluta* of yesterday will not be respected in ballet of our type; too much is required of the young dancer to-day for concentration on a few heroic rôles. A Karsavina, first of the modern ballerinas, will remain an exception and an inspiration.

The extraordinary popularity of ballet to-day cannot possibly last at its present pitch. Its greatest danger is the fact that there is not sufficient ballet of quality to supply the demand. Mushroom companies with high-sounding titles will grow up, there are already ominous signs, and once the standard is lowered ballet as a whole is bound to suffer. There can be no comparison with the theatre, which has a far larger repertoire to draw upon. The repertory ballet company writes its own plays as well as acting in them!

Meanwhile the visitors from major companies from abroad should do something to satisfy the demand and to show us our own progress in true perspective.

CONCERTS IN LONDON

George Dannatt

★

DURING the last six years we have in varying ways been sub-
jected to much propaganda. We have learned that our critical
faculties can be deadened by reiterated half-truths, and that we
must be cautious in accepting information thus put forward. In
the world of music the line has been that as a nation we have
become more musically minded. It remains to be seen whether
we should treat this information with the scepticism with which
most critics at first greeted it.

Music certainly has received its share of publicity, and there
have been some indications of awakened interest. After sitting
through a number of concerts during the last few months, up to
the end of June, one has the feeling that this next year will be a
decisive time, when we shall probably learn whether the new
audience has come to stay, or whether increased concert attendances were just another manifestation of the war-weary mind.
Will those who displayed keenness during that period of unreality
continue to do so now that the incentive to search for mental
stimulation has ceased? Large audiences have been due partly to
this need for stimulation, and partly to the fact that the need was
recognised and catered for; not only by the sponsoring of such
bodies as ENSA and CEMA in their provision of both artists
and reasonably priced seats, but by the courage and vision of
individual enterprise such as that of Myra Hess.

The interest of this much-publicised new audience has been
whetted. If it is to be held and developed, it must be fostered by
the concert-promoter in progressive programme building and
by the provision of adequate concert-halls. But that is not enough.
The concert-goer must himself co-operate by welcoming such
moves, not in blind acceptance of what is put before him, but

by learning to recognise and not tolerate incompetence, in discriminating between the vagaries of the virtuosi and the unobtrusive claims of the accomplished executant, and above all in not allowing the mass emotion of applause to sweep him off his feet.

There are at present more than fourteen orchestras in London, but not one really adequate concert-hall. The recently formed Philharmonia Orchestra made its public debut in the gloomy nonconformist atmosphere of the Kingsway Hall. There was a packed audience for this concert conducted by Sir Thomas Beecham, who favoured them with one of his tip-and-run appearances; but for the enterprising series of Chamber Concerts on Saturday afternoons, also promoted by Philharmonia, this centrally situated hall was seldom more than a quarter full. There is also generally room for many more at Boyd Neel's venturesome programmes at Chelsea Town Hall. On the same night as one of his uncrowded concerts a short distance away an immense muster of people were, with bated breath, gazing rapturously through their binoculars at Schnabel; despite this highly magnified hero worship, his reappearance was a great event.

In three Beethoven concerts, with the Philharmonia Orchestra directed by Issay Dobrowen and a welcome new-comer, Alceo Galliera, Schnabel displayed his interpretation of the complete concertos, including the uninspired and seldom-played Triple Concerto with Grumiaux and Fournier as proficient violin and 'cello soloists. As expected, Schnabel was spectacular in his complete mastery of certain points of technique, such as the quick repetition of chords in both hands, but his odd mannerism of "muffing" the end of a scale-run did not permit him to play the opening of the G major Concerto with the definitive clarity that one expects from an artist of his calibre; but his performance of this work was his best all-round interpretation. His playing has mellowed considerably, but the old Schnabel was apparent from time to time—for example, in the way he hammered out the last movement of the Emperor, which spoilt a well-nigh perfect performance under Galliera.

Dobrowen was responsible for the rather dull directing of Concertos One to Four, but his performance of the Fifth Symphony was exemplary. He took the second movement slower than is usual and thereby disclosed the full beauty of the orchestration (the 'cellos in bars 88-96, for example). It was left to Galliera in his interpretation of the Fourth Symphony to give the only superlative performance of Beethoven in the whole series. Hopes were aroused by his playing of the first movement and confirmed by his brilliant Allegro Vivace (third movement) and by his dignified and determined directing of the Triple and Emperor Concertos. By these performances he proved the mettle of this orchestra and showed that, given the right conductor, they are a masterly body of players.

The London Philharmonic Orchestra seems to thrive on showy conductors. The absurd rostrum-gyrations of their most successful guest director of the season, Victor da Sabata, would be pathetic were it not for the fact that his interpretation of southern European composers is electrifying. That romancer Berlioz recounts how he took his reactionary friend Lesueur to hear Beethoven's Fifth, and how he found him fleeing the hall, incredulous and bewildered and "unable to put on his hat because he could not find his head." The playing of this work under da Sabata was a revelation such as Lesueur must have experienced; one of those rare occasions when both conductor and orchestra are inspired enough to present an admirable performance in every respect. In later concerts Sabata proved this was no happy accident by his excellently directed "Pastoral," although he overdid the rubato, as he did again in Ravel's *Bolero*. At this concert he confirmed his southern origin by his inability to interpret Sibelius. He expressed none of the cold, austere northern qualities which the score demands, and he allowed the brass section to get away with blatantly vulgar playing.

Gregor Fitelberg displayed his competence to perform the

too rarely heard music of his countryman, Szymanowski, in the latter's stimulating Ballet-Suite, *Harnassie*. Other conductors who appeared and gave a good account of themselves with the London Philharmonic Orchestra were Leonard Bernstein and Erich Leinsdorf, whilst Tippett secured a balanced performance of his deeply moving concerto for double string orchestra in the last concert of the series.

Berlioz would have experienced difficulty in finding his own head had he heard two superb performances of his Symphonie Fantastique. The ravishing orchestral tone which *can* be extracted from this enormous conception, given the right interpreter, could never have been more successfully produced than by the Amsterdam Concertgebouw Orchestra under their permanent conductor, Van Beinum, and by the Hallé Orchestra and their conductor, Barbirolli, whose presentation was probably the more wholly satisfying; there was little to choose between the sections of each orchestra, but outstanding was the glissando flute playing of the Hallé (fourth movement, bars 9 and 18) and the drum chord playing of our Dutch visitors (third movement, last bars). Without a doubt these are two of the finest orchestras in Europe. Barbirolli spoilt a reasonably successful performance of Ravel's Second Daphnis and Chloë Suite by adding some pages which the composer had not seen fit to include.

The B.B.C. June Music Festival was a welcome event. The first public Albert Hall concert was conducted by Beecham, Barbirolli was responsible for Verdi's *Requiem* in the second concert, and the last two concerts were conducted by Boult, who, in his Beethoven concert, again displayed that sympathetic understanding which makes him a first-class director of concertos; with Szigeti as soloist, the presentation of the Violin Concerto was flawless.

Sir Adrian gave a scholarly interpretation of the Beethoven Grosse Fuge from the Opus 130 Quartet, edited for orchestral strings by Weingartner. It was opportune that this performance came two days after the first performance in England of Richard Strauss's *Metamorphosen* by the Boyd Neel Orchestra, which is an exhilaratingly moving piece of music for twenty-three strings, in one movement. Strauss incorporates into the texture the rhythm of the Eroica *Funeral March*, and the work is vaguely reminiscent of the closing-scene music in *Gotterdämmerung*, but with a tinge of the mysticism of "Die Frau ohne Schatten." After the playing and before the applause there was a moment's silence, a very welcome indication that an audience has been deeply moved. Boyd Neel must certainly repeat this work, and every musician who feels the tragedy of Germany should hear it. It is music written by a contemporary for his time (and none the worse for that) as opposed to the Grosse Fuge which so greatly transcends it, and which was written as a result of the spiritual struggles of another genius, but one who wrote for all men for all time.

Alan Bush (London String Orchestra) and Boyd Neel both possess capable string orchestras. At their concerts the serious concert-goer can hear excellently balanced and thought-out programmes enthusiastically played. In the praiseworthy Gerald Cooper series of concerts at the Wigmore Hall various distinguished chamber-music ensembles worked through the majority of Mozart's Chamber Music, and the series is to be concluded this autumn.

A most welcome event has been the return of that highly controlled and meticulous body of players, the Hungarian String Quartet. Their interpretation of Bartók's Fifth Quartet (1934) was an unforgettable exposition of the highly integrated structure of that superb work. Curiously enough, their presentation of Beethoven's Opus 130 was not wholly successful; but their playing of the Haydn "Lark" Quartet was full of the elegance which it calls for.

If that enterprising German who wrote "Britain, the Land without Music" would write on our lack of concert-halls, his research would be welcome. Meanwhile the Queen's Hall cannot be rebuilt because (it is reported) the Commissioners of Crown Lands have increased the ground rent of the site from £850 to £8,000. If the young men and women who envisage a Henry Wood Concert-hall all wrote to their M.P.s and demanded that Questions be asked in the House and that the whole matter be thoroughly investigated, instead of trying to dispose of mythical and adulatory bricks, they might help one new hall to materialise.

NORTHERN DIARY

*

Scotland : by Stewart Deas

So far as he can allow general musical interests to take the place of personal bread-and-butter problems, the musician in Scotland is at present turning over in his mind two main topics. The first is one that seems to be always with us—the question what to do about the orchestral situation; the second is the proposed International Festival of Music and Drama in Edinburgh in 1947 under Glyndebourne auspices. The two topics are not unconnected, because the attitude taken by musicians and the musical public in general to the Festival idea will largely determine the nature of its influence on music in Scotland. Rightly understood, and rightly supported by Scottish musicians (we need not trouble here about the great outside public which will come in its thousands no matter what the effect on the resident musicians is), an international festival such as that planned for Edinburgh could be of enormous value to those whose normal professional musical life is at the centre or on the fringes of the scene of the annual event. But it cannot be denied also that, wrongly understood, the whole thing might prove disastrous to whatever local enterprise happens so far to have weathered the storm.

When we come to examine, however, just what has been built up locally and what has survived, we may be driven to the conclusion, especially at this time of year, that there is, after all, little to lose in any case. During the summer months, Scotland is curiously supine musically. At one time there was simply nothing of any consequence to be heard between March and October. Now there is a great deal to be heard between these months, and most of it is of better quality than that of the performances during the winter months, but it is almost all imported. We have visits to Edinburgh and Glasgow, and other

Scottish towns, of the Hallé Orchestra, the London Philharmonic, the Liverpool Philharmonic, the Boyd Neel, the Jacques, and the New London; but all this takes place mainly because, from a musical point of view, Scotland as a whole becomes rather like the remote country towns and villages which it is the business of the Arts Council and such general music purveyors to supply with tit-bits from the master's table. Not that a magnificent institution like the Hallé—which plays for a full week in Edinburgh and three days in Glasgow—can really be called a tit-bit, but the principle of the thing is that Scotland, having little or no musical food of her own, is an obvious market for England's surplus stores.

From time to time there are tremendous stirrings of the public musical conscience, and it is realised that if there is an audience for the visitors there might also, quite conceivably, be an audience for local endeavour, provided it could reach a similar standard of achievement. But how is this to be attained? In the first place, surely, by having resident, full-time orchestras in the two chief cities of Scotland. Glasgow, for the past half-century or so, has run the orchestra known as the Scottish Orchestra, which has, in one way or another, been hired for concerts in Edinburgh and other Scottish towns. But the Scottish Orchestra has always been, and still is, a seasonal orchestra and has never known from one year to the next what its plans would be, except that they would be restricted to a certain number of concerts in Glasgow and Edinburgh (latterly four in Glasgow for every one in Edinburgh) and hurried visits to any other Scottish towns, such as Dundee, Aberdeen, Inverness, Kirkcaldy, which were able to put up a guarantee for concerts. The Scottish Orchestra's visits to Edinburgh have, in the past, often been of the highest artistic value—in the days of Henschel, Landon Ronald, Weingartner, Talich, Barbirolli and others—but they have never done anything but aggravate Edinburgh's own orchestral problem, for it should have been clear to everyone, as it was certainly clear to a few (of whom Donald Francis Tovey was the most distinguished), that a dozen orchestral concerts per year is insufficient for any self-respecting city the size of Edinburgh, and that a hired orchestra can no more give a healthy musical life to a community than a hired army can decide which of its battles are worth fighting.

In a sense, of course, the Festival idea is a continuation of the hiring policy but with this difference, that if there are a few respectable musical institutions in the town in which it takes place, they can hardly fail to benefit by the incentive to a high standard of performance which such concentrated display provides. If, then, Edinburgh has good choirs, a good orchestra, and good chamber-music players, it stands to benefit enormously from an annual event to which they could all contribute. At the moment of writing, it has little to boast of. There are rumours on all sides of far-reaching schemes, but all the customary dither of committee meetings and manifestos will take us nowhere without the will of the community to make its own music and provide opportunities for its resident musicians to develop their art to its highest level.

It is clear, I think, to most people who have thought long and seriously about the matter, and who are not swayed by purely sentimental or purely mercenary considerations, that it is high time Edinburgh and Glasgow worked out their own musical salvation separately, without rancour and without fear. Glasgow's City Fathers at present do far more for the Scottish Orchestra, so-called, than Edinburgh has ever done for any orchestra playing within its gates. Even so, Glasgow does not do enough to establish an orchestra worthy of its size and wealth, so that the withdrawal of Edinburgh's support, such as it is, for the Glasgow orchestra might at first seem a serious blow, and, to some of the older generation, a sad end to an old tradition. But in reality there would be nothing sad about the breaking of this tradition which has outlived its usefulness. Edinburgh will have to learn how to run her own music now or never.

Liverpool : by A. K. Holland

In order to understand the present position of music in Liverpool, it is necessary to glance back at the situation in the years immediately preceeding the war. In 1933 the old Philharmonic Hall, which had enjoyed an enviable reputation for the best part of a century, was burned down in a disastrous fire which left nothing but the shell. There ensued a protracted series of negotiations between the Liverpool Corporation and the Philharmonic Society in which each party tried to make up the other's mind, without success. At one point it looked as if the Corporation was prepared to build a Civic Hall on a very much grander scale than that of the old Philharmonic. But the negotiations ultimately broke down and the Philharmonic was faced with the task of rebuilding its hall out of the insurance moneys. This it succeeded in doing, in face of mounting costs, by 1939, six years after the fire. No sooner had the hall been opened and preparations for the new season set in train than the war broke out. The society was thus left to meet the uncertain future with a steadily mounting debt.

Nevertheless, with some courage, it decided to carry on, and during the first two years of the war actually gave far more concerts than it had ever given in the past. By this time the debt had reached the formidable figure of £33,000 and was still growing. In these circumstances a new attempt was made to come to terms with the Corporation, and this time a solution was found which in some respects may be regarded as no less extraordinary an achievement than the original constitution of the Society itself. The Corporation agreed, in exchange for possession of the hall (and its lettings), to pay off the Society's debt and to contribute a sum of £4,000 annually, so long as the Society gave a minimum number of concerts of the old standard, besides promoting some more popular concerts and a number of concerts for educational purposes. Nor was this all. The Society was to have the use of the hall rent free for concerts and rehearsals and was to function as managers in return for a further annual sum of £500. The value of the rent-free lease has been estimated at £1,000, but it is a very modest estimate now that the Society gives during the winter months three concerts a week, besides holding gramophone sessions and entertaining its Club members to lectures once a month.

The beauty of this arrangement was that each party was privately convinced that it had behaved with extreme generosity and that the other had made a sharp bargain. The Philharmonic has never ceased to proclaim that the £4,000 is not a subsidy, or only partly so. But nobody perhaps was more surprised than the Corporation when the Society proceeded to go into the concert business on a big scale, which increased each year. With the aid of grants from CEMA, the orchestra extended its activities outside Liverpool, and the total of its concerts rapidly rose until it has now reached something like 250 in a full year.

The new arrangement took effect in the summer of 1942, and at the same time the orchestra was reconstituted. From circumstances directly connected with the war it was able to acquire the services of some very eminent players, many of whom had been released from the B.B.C. Salon Orchestra. Most of these, with the end of the war, have now left us, but there is no doubt that from the first the orchestra set itself out to attain the highest standard. Dr. Malcolm Sargent became its principal conductor, and has remained so. Mr. Louis Cohen, whose Merseyside Symphony Orchestra formed the nucleus of the war-time orchestra, has been conceded the next largest proportion of the concerts, and for the rest there can be very few conductors in the country who have not at one time or another taken charge of the orchestra, from Sir Thomas Beecham downwards, the most recent acquisition being Mr. André Kostelanetz. All these factors of constantly changing personnel and of the impact of so many different conductors have made it difficult for the orchestra to achieve a homogeneous style and a consistent standard of playing. But at its best there is no doubt that a very pliant instrument has been created.

At the moment we are anxiously awaiting the results of the past year's trading, for the sad fact is that not even Mr. David Webster, the architect of the new Philharmonic régime, was able in the post-blitz era, when everyone went concert-mad, to make our touring orchestra pay. We await, too, the portentous new constitution of the Society, which, among many ambitious aims, takes power unto itself to give concerts "anywhere in the world" and to promote or assist in promoting a Liverpool School of Music which many feel is needed. Meanwhile, the University has got as far as proposing to create a musical professorship.

I have exhausted my space in dealing with the affairs of our principal society because it has occupied during the past six years so much of the centre of the stage. Its winter season ended, it has during recent months given some popular concerts and found itself faced with the grim ordeal of peace-time conditions, with money getting tighter and some of the benefits of the war period, such as the ENSA concerts, vanishing. For the rest, we have had some occasional concerts of the "celebrity" class. Schnabel succeeded in getting an audience of the right dimensions, but Elman and Ida Haendel were less fortunate. Some of the smaller societies which were eclipsed by the war have shown faint stirrings of life. It is certain that next season will be one of the most critical in the affairs of Liverpool music.

Manchester : by J. H. Elliott

The Hallé Orchestra, after a regrettable hiatus, has now returned to the air—and one recent occasion was marked by a miscalculation in timing that led to the finale of Brahms's First Symphony being cut off in its prime. Protests from indignant listeners—not without some rather plaintive tilts at "bureaucracy"—enlivened the correspondence columns of the *Man-*

chester Guardian for some time. It seemed to me rather futile and one-sided: any broadcast which unfortunately overruns its time (whatever the cause) must, and indeed should, be curtailed. Now, before an outraged reader seizes his pen to write to the Editor—"If your Manchester correspondent cannot see the distinction between the performance of a great symphony and a swing item or music-hall turn, he should devote his energies to rat-catching or drain-cleaning (occupations, I may add, which seem particularly well adapted to his intellectual capacity)" and so forth—let me say that of course I see the distinction and that I deplore the incident as much as any of the protestants. But the B.B.C. is under contract, as it were, to provide for widely differing tastes and should not be side-tracked by other considerations, however lofty. The best suggestion that emerged was that a margin of extra time should be allowed—to be filled up if necessary by the time-honoured gramophonic stop-gap. Yet this, in common fairness, would have to be applied to all programmes, which would make broadcasting a very scrappy affair.

On the whole, the writers would have been better employed in pressing for the speedy provision of a suitable concert-hall for the Hallé Orchestra, which, even in the Manchester area, leads a more or less nomadic life between Belle Vue on the outskirts and our local Albert Hall, which is so small that concerts there have been repeated on consecutive nights throughout the late season. The great civic reconstruction plan, it is true, allows for a palatial "home of the arts"—but this is only a fragment of ambitious plans for turning Manchester into a sort of garden paradise, and anyone who is acquainted with our city will therefore appreciate that the laying of the foundation-stone is not a probable event of the very near future. Plans have been made for providing the disembowelled Free Trade Hall with a new inside, but at the moment of writing it still remains a grim memorial to the Luftwaffe's inaccuracies in a presumed attempt to demolish a nearby railway terminus.

Another point that could have been raised was the desirability of a substantial municipal subsidy for the orchestra. This is merited, not only on pure cultural grounds, but because the Hallé Orchestra is a first-class advertisement for Manchester. During May it gave twenty-two concerts—twenty of them outside the city—in the Midlands, as far south as Bournemouth and Southampton, and as far west as Bristol. June concerts were mainly in Scotland, the overall score for the month being one home and fifteen away.

Yet, though we do not grudge sharing our orchestra—on the contrary—there is, as the Society's manager, Mr. T. E. Bean, pointed out in a recent *Radio Times* article, considerable danger in this hectic activity, at present necessary to keep the pot boiling. Half this number of concerts, plus an adequate subsidy, would be good for the orchestra's artistic health, and hence for its publicity value to the city.

The Manchester Hallé season proper ended with the Sunday Belle Vue concert on May 5th—the Eighth and Ninth Symphonies of Beethoven (the latter with the Hallé and Sheffield Philharmonic choirs). During the winter Mr. Barbirolli has given his Belle Vue audiences ten Beethoven programmes, or programmes primarily sustained by Beethoven, including all the symphonies. I have heard a few questionings about mild departures from the traditional—orchestral light and shade not quite on the "accepted" style, and so forth. Well, regard for precedent is a good thing so long as we remember that there are bad traditions as well as good ones. The whole point is whether an unorthodox touch is convincing in itself, which of course includes avoidance of any solecism of style. As far as my acquaintance with Mr. Barbirolli's Beethoven readings goes, I feel that he adds to our knowledge of the composer when he by-passes the beaten tracks.

The Hallé Pension Fund Concert, with Clifford Curzon as soloist, was devoted to Tchaikovsky; and when it was announced that members of the B.B.C. Northern Orchestra and Fairey

Aviation Works Band were to join in, making 135 players in all, some of the more nervous patrons feared that they were about to be B-flat-minored out of their wits. However, all was well: the extra brass was reserved for the climax of a brilliant performance of "1812." This was a popular and thoroughly enjoyable concert—for even the "concerto for two" (or should it be twenty million?) has proved big enough, and good enough, to survive the rigours of a Hollywood plugging. All artists taking part generously gave their services.

Edward Isaacs's Tuesday Midday Concerts carried our shockingly brief season well into May. As ever, this excellent artist and concert manager has contrived a series of recitals that has both given to his subscribers the opportunity of hearing well-known artists and to many gifted young performers the chance of a public hearing. The Tuesday series is one of the bright spots in our musical life.

Mischa Elman revisited us at the end of May after an absence of many years, bringing Leopold Mittman as his admirable partner at the piano. There was much exquisite lyrical playing in the "Spring" Sonata of Beethoven and a noble performance of Bach's *Chaconne*. Mendelssohn's Concerto (with a break between first and second movements) did not commend itself so well, despite the wonderful playing. When will violin virtuosi learn to render unto the orchestra the things that are orchestral? The violin-piano repertory is wide enough, surely, for this kind of incongruity to be avoided.

Birmingham : by John Waterhouse

Quite the most notable musical event in Birmingham during the past three months has been the sudden blossoming of a hither-to obscure bud called The Midland Music Makers. At first rumour, their proposal to produce *Prince Igor* on the small and scantily equipped stage of the Midland Institute seemed crazy. *Prince Igor* demands spectacle, and spectacle means a crowded stage, gorgeous costumes, complex lighting, and elaborate scenery. Well, the first three were there in abundance. Surely no stage can ever have been quite so crowded as was this in the Prologue, where movement seemed possible only by a process of individual rotation, elbows as cogs, yet all was under control. In the Polovtsi camp four gallant archers lashed the tottering stage into clouds of dust within the few square feet allotted to them. The costumes were an honourable triumph over the Board of Trade. As for the lighting, one could only wonder how it was done, and occasional disconcerting appearances of sudden "spots" on stomachs were no doubt corrected after the first night. The simple décor, too, was very effective, including the bit of flame that popped up from behind a wall in the tocsin scene. The choral singing was good, and the orchestra had few dangerous moments. Arthur Street conducted with admirable authority. Act III was omitted (Konchak's battle-song and part of the march were inserted into Act II); but we really did hear and see *Prince Igor*, and it was an experience for which to be profoundly grateful. I missed the Bournville Works Musical Society's presentation of Stanford's *The Travelling Companion*—another interesting and enterprising choice— but heard well of it.

The City Orchestra continues to give many fine performances, though both the players and their conductor, George Weldon, sometimes show signs of the overwork entailed by their many educational duties and outside concerts. Mr. Weldon repeatedly shows himself especially a master in the building up of large structures, and in the holding together of those which, like the Elgar A flat Symphony, are apt to creak and come apart if left to themselves. But he has also fashioned many small things exquisitely. The programme committee cannot be so warmly commended. One complains not only of the dearth of modern music on the bills: much criticism has already been directed against that locally, and may eventually have its effect. That problem-child the new musical public must, indeed, be plentifully supplied with the classics which it is only just learning to know; and, maybe, frequently cosseted with extra doses of Tchaikovsky. But why is it not encouraged to know and to develop its taste on a wider range of the classics? In one-hundred-and-seventy-odd Thursday and Sunday programmes during the past two years we have had, for example, only four different Haydn symphonies. Plebiscite has twice acclaimed (with promising taste) *The Hebrides* as the most popular of overtures; yet never a *Meerestille* or a *Melusina*. Why, again, when Mr. Weldon shapes the Seventh Symphony of Sibelius so magnificently, has he not yet been asked to give us the fourth or the sixth? And so on with the other great names. Two excuses one hears are: (*a*) Box-office. This would be more acceptable if the ordinary observer could see any evidence that the presence of Tchaikovsky always filled the house, while the presence of a contemporary work or a less familiar classic always emptied it. (*b*) That the programmes of other orchestras are equally unenterprising—a miserable excuse. However, on the credit side we have recently welcomed, among modern works, Rubbra's superb Third Symphony (received with an enthusiasm which hardly endorsed the committee's general policy), Vaughan Williams's Fifth Symphony (second performance here), Walton's Symphony (this at least now seems established in our repertoire), and his *Sinfonia Concertante*; and among rather less-familiar classics, the First Symphony of Dvořák.

The orchestra's liaison with the city education authorities (musical adviser, Dr. Desmond Macmahon) seems to be working efficiently and fruitfully in school visits and youth concerts. A huge City Orchestra Club flourishes. And two recent portents are at least equally significant for the future of music in Birmingham: the sensationally rapid organisation of an Industrial Music Club, with foci in countless factories, under the sponsorship of the Arts Council; and a hum of gathering activity from the Midland Institute School of Music, under the new directorship of Dr. Christopher Edmunds.

Aloft at the Town Hall organ every Wednesday lunch-hour, G. D. Cunningham continues adown the years to set for our Birmingham music its most continuously high standard of execution and musicianship. As conductor of the City Choir Dr. Cunningham provided in April a grand performance of Verdi's *Requiem*. Here the city's orchestra joined its choir as a few weeks earlier the choir had joined the orchestra under Mr. Weldon in twin productions of Beethoven's Ninth Symphony. This double performance of the Ninth, Thursday and Sunday, may, we hope, become an annual event. At a lower level of execution, but deserving of very honourable mention (for through sincere and decent second-class performances the main life-stream of music will always flow and the musical health of a place be tested), was the Choral Union's *St. Matthew Passion*, with Appleby Matthews, on Good Friday.

Among the new musical public chamber music still seems, alas, to be a dog with a bad name; and it has recently lost its most faithful and lovable Birmingham champion in the late Johann C. Hock. But three active societies effectively support its cause: the Midland Music Club, the Ridgdowne Music Club, and the University Musical Society. And the Barber Institute Concerts, long postponed by the war, are now well under way, directed with energy and enterprise by Professor J. A. Westrup. At one of these a most glorious and impeccable performance of Schubert's G major Quartet (a neglected masterpiece if ever there was one) will remain a glowing memory for all who journeyed out to hear it. The players were the New Hungarian Quartet. Among other recent distinguished visitors to the city may be mentioned Schnabel, Mischa Elman, Szigeti; and the Hallé Orchestra, supporting the present curious Mahler *putsch* with a de luxe performance of *Das Lied von der Erde*.

BRITISH MUSIC OF OUR TIME

Edited by A. L. Bacharach

An introductory chapter on the nineteenth-century origins of contemporary British music is followed by essays on the work of individual composers—Delius, Holst, Peter Warlock, Frank Bridge, Vaughan Williams, Ireland, Arnold Bax, Eugene Goossens, Walton, Bliss, Lambert, Moeran, Rubbra, and Britten—and some remarks on their fellow-workers, with an analysis of future trends.

A SURVEY OF RUSSIAN MUSIC

M. D. Calvocoressi

Chapters on the early history of music in Russia, Opera and the special features of Russian music, Mussorgsky, Rimsky-Korsakof, Tchaikovsky, and the other pre-Revolution composers, Stravinsky, Prokofief, Music under the Soviets, the National schools of the Union republics, and Russian composers who have worked abroad.

MUSIC IN ENGLAND

Eric Blom

A discussion of English musical life from its beginnings to the present day, setting the scene in which music has unfolded itself, not only through the activities of composers, but also those of performers, scholars, and institutions.

BALLET

Arnold Haskell

A complete guide to Ballet in pocket form: its history, its theory, notes on the leading personalities and creators of modern Ballet, studies of individual ballets and of some contemporary dancers, illustrated with photogravure plates and decorations by Kay Ambrose.